SPEAK JAPANESE WITH CONFIDENCE!

ESSENTIAL JAPANESE

PHRASEBOOK & DICTIONARY

Excuse me, where is Harajuku station?
Sumimasen, Harajuku no eki wa doko des-ka?

It's that way, straight ahead and then turn right.
Sono michi o, mas-sugu it-tay, sorekara migi ni magat-tay kuda-sai.

Thank you very much.
Dohmo arigatoh gozai-mas.

TUTTLE Pu...

Tokyo | Rutland, Vermont | Singapore

Contents

Introduction

Welcome to the Tuttle Essential Language series, covering all of the most popular Asian languages. These books are basic guides to communicating in the language. They're concise, accessible and easy to understand, and you'll find them indispensable on your trip abroad to get you where you want to go, pay the right prices and do everything you're planning to do.

This guide is divided into 14 themed sections and starts with a pronunciation table which explains the phonetic pronunciation of all the words and sentences you'll need to know, and a basic grammar guide which will help you construct basic sentences in the language. At the end of the book is an extensive English–Japanese dictionary.

Throughout the book you'll come across boxes with a 👆 symbol beside them. These are designed to help you if you can't understand what your listener is saying to you. Hand the book over to them and encourage them to point to the appropriate answer to the question you are asking.

Other boxes in the book—this time without the 👆 symbol— give listings of themed words with their English translations beside them.

For extra clarity, we have put all phonetic pronunciations of the foreign language terms in italic.

This book covers all topics you are likely to come across during the course of a visit, from reserving a room for the night to ordering food and drink at a restaurant and what to do if you lose your credit cards and money. With over 2,000 commonly used words and essential sentences at your fingertips you can rest assured that you will be able to get by in all situations, so let **Essential Japanese** become your passport to learning to speak with confidence!

Pronunciation guide

Japanese is very easy to pronounce. It is made up of strings of syllables (**a**, **ka**, **ta**, etc.) which join together following very simple rules of pronunciation (e.g., **anata** is pronounced *a-na-ta*). Each syllable has mostly even stress and combinations of vowels do not represent completely new sounds but are pronounced as two separate vowels in succession (**ei**=**e-i**, **ai**=**a-i**, **ao**=**a-o**, etc.).

Vowels

Japanese has five vowels, pronounced either long or short. The long vowels are basically the same vowel sound pronounced twice, as **i-i**, **o-o**, etc. This book uses a close English approximation of the long vowel to write the sound (e.g., **oo** is written **oh** and **aa** becomes **ah**, etc). The meaning of the word is altered by the length of the vowel sound, e.g., **ojisan** = 'middle-aged man' as compared to **ojisan** = 'an old man'. Note that a final **e** is always pronounced (e.g., sak**e**, 'rice wine', is pronounced close to *sakay*).

a	like **a** in **A**merica	*asa*	morning
aa	long **aa** written as **ah** (pronounced like the exclamation Ahh!)	*mah*	"Oh dear"
e	like **e** in p**e**t or sometimes like **ay** in sw**ay** but shorter	*des* *saké*	is liquor
ee	long **ee** written as **eh**, like **ere** in th**ere**	*eh-to-nay*	"Well, then"
i	like **i** in p**i**t, though slightly longer	*nichi*	day
ii	long **ii** written as **ee**, like **ee** in k**ee**p	*ee-ye*	"Yeah"
o	like **o** as in t**o**p	*yoru*	night
oo	long **oo** written as **oh**, like **ou** in f**ou**r but longer	*kyoh*	big
u	like **u** as in p**u**t	*haru*	spring (season)
uu	long **uu** written as **oo**, like **oo** as in h**oo**p	*choomon*	medium

Note: When **i** or **u** come between two consonants or at the end of a word, they are shortened and often not pronounced at all (e.g., **desu** becomes *des* and **mimashita** becomes *mimashta*).

Vowel combinations

When two vowels appear next to each other in a word, each vowel is pronounced separately. The most common combinations are:

ai	**a-i** as in d**ai**s	*hai*	yes
ao	**a-o** as in n**ow**	*nao*	still
ei	**e-i** as in d**ei**ty	*rei*	example
ue	**u-e** as in fl**ue**nt	*ue*	up

Consonants

Most Japanese consonants are similar in pronunciation to English.

b	**b** as in **b**at	*bin*	a bottle
ch	**ch** as in **ch**ip	*nichi*	day
d	**d** as in **d**ay	*damay*	not good
f	**f** as in **f**ood	*fu-yu*	winter
g	**g** as in **g**ive	*gogo*	afternoon
h	**h** as in **h**at	*haru*	spring (season)
j	**j** as in **j**ump	*niji*	two o'clock
k	**k** as in **k**ing	*koko*	here
m	**m** as in **m**at	*totemo*	very much
n	**n** as in **n**ut;	*nama-e*	name
p	**p** as in **p**at	*pos-to*	post
r	Somewhere between English **r**, **l** and **d**. Never rolled **r**; more like **r** in ca**r**	*rai-gets*	next month
s	**s** as in **s**tart	*semetay*	at least
sh	**sh** as in **sh**ip	*shi-o*	salt
t	**t** as in **t**ip	*doh-shtay*	why
ts	**ts** as in hi**ts**	*its*	when
w	**w** as in **w**att	*wakaru*	understand
y	**y** as in **y**es	*yoru*	night
z	**z** as in **z**oo	*mizu*	water

Basic grammar

1 Sentence construction

The greatest difference between Japanese and English sentences is the position of the verb in the sentence. In Japanese sentences the verb always comes at the end, so the basic structure is **subject +object+verb**:

Watashi wa   *sushi o*   *tabemashita*

I (subject)   sushi (object)   eat (past tense) = I ate sushi.

2 Parts of speech

Nouns Japanese nouns have no articles and no plural forms. *Zasshi* (magazine), for example, could mean "a/the magazine", "magazines", or "the/some magazines". To indicate a quantity of an object, Japanese uses a number plus a counting word (see pages 17 and 18).

Pronouns Japanese uses pronouns far less than in English. They are in fact often omitted. In English we have to specify who went by using a pronoun in the sentence "I went to Omotesando yesterday". In Japanese you can merely say *Kinoh Omotesando e ikimashita* (yesterday to-Omotesando went), in which the person who went is implied from the context. The most frequently used pronouns in Japanese are *watashi* (I) and *anata* (you). The pronouns "he", "she" and "they" are used less often.

Adjectives Like in English, Japanese can use adjectives in two ways, before the noun they describe (*mushi-atswee hi*, a **humid** day) or following it (*kyoh wa mushi-atswee desu*, today is **humid**). In grammatical terms, adjectives can in fact function like verbs, and have tenses like verbs (see below).

Verbs The verb is the most important element in the Japanese sentence, since it is quite possible for a sentence to consist of just a verb and not much else:

Tabemasen-ka?   Would you like to eat?

Tabemashita.   I ate (already).

Various different suffixes are added to verbs to indicate negative forms, tenses, and levels of politeness.

In Japanese, honorific verb endings are used to show respect for the person you are speaking to. There are three basic levels of politeness: the plain or informal; the polite or formal; and the honorific or highly formal. If you look up a verb in the dictionary you will find it written in the base, or plain form: for example, *taberu* (to eat), *iku* (to go) or *miru* (to see). This is the form used in informal conversation, so, for example, you might say to a friend *Ashita ee restoran ni iku* (tomorrow I-to a good restaurant-am going).

However, when you talk to people you have only just met or to someone more senior than you, add the polite ending **-masu** to the verb. For example, *Ashita ee restoran ni ikimasu*. The **-masu** ending indicates the medium polite or formal level. The honorific or highly formal level is used when someone wishes to show extreme politeness, either because of their own humble position (a shop assistant to a customer, for example) or because of the exalted nature of the person (like a company president) he or she is speaking to. In this phrasebook, the informal level has been used in close personal situations, the medium polite or formal level is used in general conversation, and the honorific only when showing how someone in a service situation might address you.

Japanese tenses are fairly simple. The **future tense** has the same form as the present, so that *tabemasu* "I am eating" could mean "I eat" or "I will eat". The **past tense** is shown by adding the suffix **ta**: *tabemashita* (I ate), *mimashita* (I saw). The only other form used for tense is the **continuing action form**, made using the suffix **te**: *tabete imasu* (I am continuing to eat); *tabete imashita* (I was eating). English speakers may find the lack of other tenses confusing, but Japanese employs other non-verbal forms to express them.

The **negative** is made by adding the suffix -**nai** to the plain form of the verb, for example, *tabenai* (I do not eat), or the suffix **n** to the polite **masu** ending, for example, *tabemasen* (I do not eat).

3 Male and female speech

Most phrases and sentences in this book are given in a gender-neutral form but you should be aware that males and females often use different pronouns and sentence endings. Sometimes these different phrases are given in the book (See pages 43-45) and are indicated by [Female] and [Male] before the phrase.

4 Relationship Words (particles)

English uses word order to indicate relationships: "the dog bit the man" and "the man bit the dog" are different because of the order in which the words appear. In Japanese, short connecting words known as "particles" are used to show the relationships between words. The doer of an action (the subject) is shown by adding the particle *ga* or *wa* after it. The receiver of the action (the object) is shown by adding the particle *o* after it. For example:

Inu   *ga* *hito*   *o* *kanda.*
the dog (subject) the man (object) bit
= The dog bit the man.

Hito   *ga* *inu*   *o* *kanda.*
the man (subject) the dog (object) bit
= The man bit the dog.

Japanese has another particle, *wa*, which often marks the subject as well. This has the function of pointing out a particular word and emphasizing that this is the main topic of the sentence. It is like the English phrase "as for".

Kono seki   *wa*   *aite imasu*   *ka?*
this seat   (as for=subject) free   question marker
= Is this seat free?

Anata   *wa*   *sushi* *o*   *tabemasen-ka?*
You   (as for=subject) sushi (object) ate (question marker)
= Did you eat sushi?

The examples above also show the use of the question-making particle *ka*. This is used at the end of a sentence just like a question mark, to turn the sentence into a question. Another important particle is *no*, used to join two nouns together to indicate the possessive (similar to 's in English).

Watashi	*no*	*Yuki*	*des.*
I	(possessive particle)	Yuki	is

= I am Yuki.

Aiko	*no*	*kaban*	*desu.*
Aiko	(possessive particle)	bag	is

= It is Aiko's bag.

Aygo	*no*	*menyoo wa*	*arimas*	*ka?*
English	(possessive)	menu (subject)	is there	question marker

=Do you have an English menu?

Other particles act like English prepositions: *ni* (at, in, on, to), *e* (to a place), *de* (at, with), *kara* (from), *made* (to, until), and *yori* (from). These are always placed after the word they refer to:

aki ni	**in** autumn
Tokyo e	**to** Tokyo
magari-kado de	**at** the corner
Shinjuku kara Shibuya made	**from** Shinjuku **to** Shibuya
tomodachi yori moraimashita	received **from** a friend

Kara and *yori* "from" can be used interchangeably for actions and time, although *kara* is more commonly used. *Yori* is also used to compare two nouns, similar to the English "than".

5 Some useful grammatical forms

Here are some useful sentence patterns that will help you to form new sentences using words in this book.

Please When you want to ask someone for something, add *onegai shimasu* "Please could I have" after the thing you would like. This is a useful phrase that can be used in a variety of ways. To ask for something in a shop or restaurant, say what it is followed by *onegai shimasu*:

*Hon **onegai shimasu**.*	A book, please.
*Pan **onegai shimasu**.*	Some bread, please.

It can also be used to mean "Yes, please" when someone offers you something, e.g., "Would you like this?" ***Onegai shimasu*** "Yes, please".

Useful verbs Two very useful verbs are **desu** (often shortened to **des)**, equivalent to "is/are" and **arimasu** (often shortened to *arimas*), "there is/there are":

*Watashi wa Amerika-jin **des***.	I **am** American.
*Kyoh wa gets-yohbi **des***.	Today **is** Monday.
*Kono wa Shinjuku **des***.	This **is** Shinjuku.
*Kono wa Shinjuku **des**-ka?*	**Is** this Shinjuku?
*Aita heya wa **arimas**-ka?*	**Are there** any vacancies?
*Toiray wa doko ni **arimas**-ka?*	**Is there** a bathroom?

Please do something To ask someone to do something, add the verb **-te kuda-sai** (*-te kuda-sai*) (Note that the verb ending **-ru** is dropped.

taberu (to eat)	**Tabete kuda-sai.**	Please eat.
miseru (to show)	**Misete kuda-sai.**	Please show me.
kuru (to come)	**Kite kuda-sai.**	Please come.

To ask someone not to do something, add the negative form **nai-de kuda-sai** to the verb.

taberu	**Tabenai-de kuda-sai.**	Please don't eat.
miseru	**Misenai-de kuda-sai.**	Please don't show me.
kuru	**Konai-de kuda-sai.**	Please don't come.

6 A final tip

The Japanese language is full of loanwords, most of them from English. They are used for the name of things, and many English nouns therefore have a close Japanese equivalent. If you get stuck for a word, try pronouncing the English word slowly in a Japanese way. For example, if you pronounce "bus station" syllable by syllable, *ba-su su-tay-shon*, this will turn out to be a perfectly understandable Japanese word!

7 The Japanese writing system

Written Japanese combines three different kinds of characters: *hiragana*, *katakana* and *kanji*. *Hiragana* are the 46 alphabetic letters used to write grammatical elements in a Japanese sentence, like verbs, particles and verb endings. *Katakana* are a parallel set of 46 letters used to write foreign words.

The other components of a sentence are written using *kanji* (Chinese characters), that is: nouns, adjectives, some adverbs and the base forms of some verbs.

Place names on station notice boards are usually written in *kanji*, but the pronunciation in *hiragana* is also given underneath the *kanji*. In the large cities, the pronunciation in the Latin alphabet (*romaji*, "Roman letters") will also appear. *Kanji* characters provide the underlying meanings of words. For example, the *kanji* for To-kyo means "eastern capital", O-saka means "great slope", Hane-da means "field of wings" and Roppon-gi means "six trees".

In this book, Japanese script forms of all the phrases are given so that you can show these to a Japanese person in case they don't understand what you are saying. If you are interested in learning the Japanese script, there are small books you can buy to do so.

1. The Basics

1.1 Personal details

In Japan the family name precedes the given name, which is followed by a title. The title *-san* (Mr, Mrs and Ms.) can be attached either to the surname or the given name. Small children are addressed by their given name plus *-chan*, and boys by either their given name (among friends) or their surname (at school, for example) plus *-kun*. Subordinates in companies may be addressed by their surname plus *-kun*. Anyone regarded as an intellectual is called **sensei** (*sen-say*, 'teacher').

your name	*o-nama-e* お名前
my name/given name(s)	*nama-e* 名前
surname	*say* 姓
address	*joo-sho* 住所
postal code (zip code)	*yoobin bangoh* 郵便番号
sex (gender)	*say-bets* 性別
male	*dan* 男
female	*dan* 女
nationality	*koku-seki* 国籍
date of birth	*say-nen-gappi* 生年月日

place of birth	*shushoh-chi* 出生地
occupation	*shoku-gyoh* 職業
married	*ki-kon* 既婚
single	*mi-kon* 未婚
divorced	*ri-kon* 離婚
(number of) children	*ko-domo (no kazu)* 子供（の数）
passport	*pasu-pohto (ryo-ken)* パスポート（旅券）
identity card	*mibun shoh-may-sho* 身分証明書
driving license number	*men-kyo-shoh bangoh* 運転免許証番号

1.2 Today or tomorrow?

What day is it today?	*Kyoh wa nan-yohbi des-ka?* 今日は何曜日ですか？
Today's Monday.	*Kyoh wa Gets-yohbi des.* 今日は月曜日です。
Today's Tuesday.	*Kyoh wa Ka-yohbi des.* 今日は火曜日です。
Today's Wednesday.	*Kyoh wa Swee-yohbi des.* 今日は水曜日です。
Today's Thursday.	*Kyoh wa Moku-yohbi des.* 今日は木曜日です。
Today's Friday.	*Kyoh wa Kin-yohbi des.* 今日は金曜日です。
Today's Saturday.	*Kyoh wa Do-yohbi des.* 今日は土曜日です。
Today's Sunday.	*Kyoh wa Nichi-yohbi des.* 今日は日曜日です。
What's the date today?	*Kyoh wa nan-gats nan-nichi des-ka?* 今日は何月何日ですか？
in January	*Ichi-gats-ni* 一月に

since February	*Ni-gats-kara* 二月から
in spring	*haru-ni* 春に
in summer	*natsu-ni* 夏に
in autumn	*aki-ni* 秋に
in winter	*fuyu-ni* 冬に
2017	*Ni-sen joo-shichi nen* 2017年
the twenty-first century	*nijoo-is-say-ki* 21世紀
What's the date today?	*Kyoh wa nan-nichi des-ka?* 今日は何日ですか?
Today's the 24th.	*Kyoh wa nijoo-yokka des.* 今日は24日です。
Monday	*Gets-yohbi* 月曜日
3 November 2017	*Ni-sen joo-shichi nen joo-ichi-gats mikka* 2017年11月3日
in the morning	*asa ni* 朝に
in the afternoon	*gogo ni* 午後に
in the evening	*yoogata ni* 夕方に
at night	*yoru ni* 夜に
this morning	*kesa* 今朝
this afternoon	*kyoh no gogo* 今日の午後
this evening	*kyoh no yoogata* 今日の夕方
tonight	*kom-ban* 今晩
last night	*saku-ban* 昨晩
yesterday	*kinoh* 昨日
tomorrow	*ashta* 明日
this week	*kon-shoo* 今週
next month	*rai-gets* 来月
last year	*kyo-nen* 去年

next...	*tsugi no* 次の
in...days	*...nichi de* …日で
in...weeks	*...shookan de* …週間で
in...months	*...ka-getsu de* …か月で
in...years	*...nenkan de* …年間で
...weeks ago	*...shookan ma-e-ni* …週間前に
day off	*kyoo-jitsu* 休日

1.3 What time is it?

What time is it now?	*Ima nan-ji des-ka?* 今何時ですか?
It's nine o'clock.	*(Gozen) ku-ji des.* (午前) 9時です。
It's five past ten (am).	*(Gozen) joo-ji go-fun des.* (午前) 10時5分です。
It's a quarter past eleven (am).	*(Gozen) joo-ichi-ji joo-go-fun des.* (午前) 11時15分です。
It's twenty past twelve (pm).	*(Gogo) joo-ni-ji ni-jup-pun des.* (午後) 12時20分です。
It's half past one (pm).	*(Gogo) ichi-ji han des.* (午後) 1時半です。
It's twenty-five to three (pm).	*(Gogo) ni-ji san-joo-go-fun des.* (午後) 2時35分です。
It's a quarter to four (pm).	*(Gogo) san-ji yon-joo-go-fun des.* (午後) 3時45分です。
It's ten to five (pm).	*(Gogo) yo-ji go-jup-pun des.* (午後) 4時50分です。
It's 12pm.	*Joo-ni-ji des.* 12時です。
It's noon.	*Shoh-go des.* 正午です。
It's midnight.	*Yo-naka no joo-ni-ji des.* 夜中の12時です。
30 minutes	*san-jup-pun-kan* 三十分間

What time?	*Nan-ji?* 何時？
What time can I come by?	*Nan-ji ni kureba ee des-ka?* 何時に来れば いいですか？
at...	*... ni* …に
after...	*... sugi-ni* …過ぎに
before...	*... ma-e-ni* …前に
between...and...	*... to ... no aida-ni...* …と…の間に
from...to...	*... kara ... maday* …から…まで
in...minutes	*... fun go-ni* …分後に
in an hour	*ichi-jikan go ni* 1時間後に
in hours	*... jikan go-ni* …時間後に
in 15 minutes	*joo-go-fun go-ni* 15分後に
in 45 minutes	*yon-joo-go-fun go-ni* 45分後に
early	*haya-sugi-mas* 早過ぎます
late	*oso-sugi-mas* 遅過ぎます
on time	*mani-at-tay/... ni mani-a-imas* 間に合って／…に間に合います
I will be a little bit late.	*Sukoshi okuremas.* 少し遅れます。
I am sorry I am late.	*Okurete sumimasen.* 遅れてすみません。

1.4 Numbers and counting

There are two ways to count objects in Japanese. One is to use a normal number (1, 2, 3 etc) followed by a counting word, e.g., one "sheet" of paper, two "glasses" of beer. For up to 10 objects, you can just use the item numbers, e.g., "one item"= *hitots*, "two items"= *futats*, etc. Thus, two hamburgers would be *hambagah futats*.

Normal Numbers	Native Japanese
1 *ichi* 一	1 *hi-tots* 一つ
2 *ni* 二	2 *fu-tats* 二つ
3 *san* 三	3 *mits* 三つ
4 *shi/yon* 四	4 *yots* 四つ
5 *go* 五	5 *i-tsuts* 五つ
6 *roku* 六	6 *mutts* 六つ
7 *shichi/nana* 七	7 *na-nats* 七つ
8 *hachi* 八	8 *yatts* 八つ
9 *ku/kyoo* 九	9 *koko-nots* 九つ
10 *joo/ju* 十	10 *toh* 十つ

Some of the most common counting words are:

台 *dai* (for machines like cars and bikes): *jitensha ichi-dai* (one bicycle), *jidosha ni-dai* (two cars)

杯 *hai* (cups): *koh-hee ni-pai* (two cups of coffee), *o-cha go-pai* (five cups of tea)

本 *hon* (for cylindrical objects, like chopsticks, cigarettes, etc.): *pen ip-pon* (one pen), *ki ni-hon* (two trees), *tabako sam-bon* (three sticks of cigarettes)

0 *ray/zero* 零	200 *ni-hyaku* 二百
11 *joo-ichi* 十一	300 *sam-byaku* 三百
31 *san-joo-ichi* 三十一	400 *yon-hyaku* 四百
32 *san-joo-ni* 三十二	500 *go-hyaku* 五百
40 *yon-joo* 四十	600 *rop-pyaku* 六百
50 *go-joo* 五十	700 *nana-hyaku* 七百
60 *roku-joo* 六十	800 *hap-pyaku* 八百
70 *nana-joo* 七十	900 *kyoo-hyaku* 九百
80 *hachi-joo* 八十	1000 *sen/issen* 千
90 *kyoo-joo* 九十	1100 *sen hyaku* 千百
100 *hyaku* 百	2000 *ni-sen* 二千
101 *hyaku ichi* 百一	3000 *san-zen* 三千
110 *hyaku joo* 百十	8000 *has-sen* 八千
120 *hyaku ni-joo* 百二十	

10,000 *ichi-man* 一万
20,000 *ni-man* 二万
100,000 *joo-man* 十万
a million *hyaku-man* 百万
one hundred million *ichi-oku* 一億

1st *dai-ichi* 第一		once *ichi-bai* 一倍
2nd *dai-ni* 第二		twice *ni-bai* 二倍
3rd *dai-san* 第三		thrice *sam-bai* 三倍

half *ham-bun* 半分
a quarter *yon-bun no ichi* 四分の一
a third *sam-bun no ichi* 三分の一
a couple, a few, some *iku-ts ka no* いくつかの
$2 + 4 = 6$ *ni tas yon wa roku* 2たす4は6
$4 - 2 = 2$ *yon hiku ni wa ni* 4ひく2は2
$2 \times 4 = 8$ *ni kakeru yon wa hachi* 2かける4は8
$4 \div 2 = 2$ *yon waru ni wa ni* 4割る2は2
odd *ki-soo no* 奇数の
even *goo-soo no* 偶数の
total *zem-bu (de)* 全部〔で〕
6m (width in meters) x 9m (height) *yoko roku meh-toru tate kyoo meh-toru* 縦6メートル、横9メートル

1.5 The weather

Is the weather going to be good?	*Ee tenki ni narimas-ka?* いい天気になりますか？
Is the weather going to be bad?	*Waru-i tenki ni narimas-ka?* 悪い天気になりますか？
Is it going to get colder?	*Samuku narimas-ka?* 寒くなりますか？
Is it going to get hotter?	*Atsuku narimas-ka?* 暑くなりますか？
What's the weather going to be like today?	*Kyoh no tenki wa doh des-ka?* 今日の天気はどうですか？
What's the weather going to be like tomorrow?	*Ashta no tenki wa doh des-ka?* 明日の天気はどうですか？

Is it going to rain?	*Amay ni narimas-ka?* 雨になりますか?
Is there going to be a storm?	*Arashi ni narimas-ka?* 嵐になりますか?
Is it going to snow?	*Yuki ni narimas-ka?* 雪になりますか?
Is it going to freeze?	*Kohri ga harimas-ka?* 氷が張りますか?
Nice breeze.	*Ee kaze des-ne.* いい風ですね。
Is there going to be a thunderstorm?	*Rai-u ni narimas-ka?* 雷雨になりますか?
Is it going to be foggy?	*Kiri ga tachimas-ka?* 霧が立ちますか?
The weather's changing.	*Tenki ga kuzuremas.* 天気がくずれます。
It's cooling down.	*Suzushiku narimas.* 涼しくなります。
What temperature is it going to be?	*Kion(g) wa nando gura-i deshoh-ka?* 気温は何度ぐらいでしょうか?

chilly **hada-zamui** 肌寒い	stormy **arashi** 嵐	heat wave **kokusho** 酷暑	squalls **sukohru** スコール
clear **kaisei** 快晴	hot **atswee** 暑い	sunny **hiatari no yoi** 日当りのよい	snow **yuki** 雪
cloudy **kumori** 曇	typhoon **taifoo** 台風	thunderstorm **raiu** 雷雨	hail **hyoh** ひょう
cold **samui** 寒い	mild **odayaka** 穏やか	wet **uten** 雨天	warm **atatakai** 暖かい
damp **shimeppoi** 湿っぽい	muggy **mushi-atswee** 蒸し暑い	wind **kaze** 風	sleet **mizore** 霙
overcast **donyori shita** どんよりした	drizzle **kirisame** 霧雨	windy **kaze no aru** 風のある	rain **ame** 雨

rainy season	fine	scorching hot	fog
tsuyu	*ee tenki*	*mohsho*	*kiri*
梅雨	いい天気	猛暑	霧
strong wind	shower	...degrees (above/ below zero)	frost
tsuyoi kaze	*niwaka-ame*	*(hyohtenka)...do*	*shimo*
強い風	にわか雨	(氷点くだ) …度	霜
light	moderate		
kasuka-na	*odayaka-na*		
かすかな	おだやかな		

1.6 Here, there...

See also 5.1 Asking directions

here	*koko* ここ
there (near to you)	*soko* そこ
there (further away)	*a-soko* あそこ
somewhere	*doko-ka* どこか
nowhere	*doko ni mo...nai* どこにも…ない
everywhere	*doko ni demo* どこにでも
far away	*toh-i* 遠い
nearby	*chi-kai* 近い
right	*migi no hoh ni* 右の方に＝
left	*hidari no hoh ni* 左の方に
to the right of	*... no migi ni* …の右に
to the left of	*... no hidari ni* …の左に
straight ahead	*mas-sugu* 真っ直ぐ
via	*... kay-yu de* …経由で
in	*... no naka ni* …の中に
on	*... no u-e ni* …の上に
under	*... no shta ni* …の下に

against	*... ni tai-shtay* …に対して
opposite	*... no mukoh-gawa ni* …の向こう側に
next to	*... no tonari ni* …の隣に
near	*... no soba ni* …の側に
in the center of	*... no man-naka ni* …の真ん中に
forward	*ma-e ay* 前へ
down	*shta ay* 下へ
up	*u-e ay* 上へ
inside	*naka ay* 中へ
outside	*soto ay* 外へ
at the front	*ma-e ni* 前に
in front of	*no ma-e ni* の前に
at the back	*ushiro ni* 後に
behind	*ushiro ay* 後へ
in the north	*kita no hoh ni* 北の方に
to the south	*minami no hoh ay* 南の方へ
from the west	*nishi no hoh kara* 西の方から
from the east	*hi-gashi no hoh kara* 東の方から

1.7 What does that sign say?

禁煙／喫煙禁止 **Kin'en/Kitsu-en kinshi** No Smoking	押／引く **Osu/Hiku** Push/pull	営業中 **Eigyoh-choo** Open
マナーモードに設定してください。 **Manah-mohdo ni settay shtay kuda-sai.** Put cell phone on silent mode.	手をふれないでください。 **Te o furenaide kuda-sai.** Please do not touch.	起こさないでください。 **Okosanaide kuda-sai.** Do not disturb.

携帯電話の通話はご遠慮く
ださい。
*Kay-tai denwa no tsoowa wa
go-enryo kuda-sai.*
Do not use cell phone(s)
here.

緊急出口／非常口
Kinkyoo deguchi/Hijoh-guchi
Emergency exit

お会計／お支払。
O-kaikei/O-shiharai.
Pay here.

避難階段／非常階段
Hinan/Hijoh kaidan
Fire escape

通行禁止
Tsookoh kinshi
No thoroughfare

セール
Sehru
Sale

セ売出し
Uridashi
Clearance

営業時間
Eigyoh jikan
Opening hours

停留所／バス停
Tay-ryoo-jo/Bas-tei
Bus stop

緊急ブレーキ／非常ブレーキ
Kinkyoo burayki/Hijoh burayki
Emergency brake

予約済
Yoyaku-zumi
Reserved

待合室
Machiai-shits
Waiting room

私有地
Shiyoo-chi
Private (property)

受付
Uketske
Reception

故障中
Koshoh choo
Out of order

足くだ注意
Ashimoto chooi
Watch your step

頭上注意
Zujoh chooi
Low clearance

エスカレー ター
Esukaraytah
Escalator

エレベーター
Erebehtah
Elevator

応急手当
Ohkyoo-teate
First aid

ペット禁止
Petto kinshi
No pets allowed

準備中
Jumbi-choo
Closed

入口
Iriguchi
Entrance

出口
Deguchi
Exit

階段
Kaidan
Stairs

銀行
Ginkoh
Bank

切符
Kippu
Tickets

窓口
Madoguchi
Counter

...階
...kai
..floor

喫煙
Kitsu-en
Smoking

注意
Chooi
Warning

警察署
Keisats-sho
Police station

郵便箱／ポスト **Yoobin-bako/posuto** Post box	撮影禁止 **Sats-ei kinshi** No photographs	危険 **Kiken** Danger
猛犬注意。 **Mohken chooi.** Beware of the dog.	タクシー乗り場 **Takushee noriba** Taxi stand	案内 **An'nai** Information
郵便物／メール **Yoobin-buts/May-ru** Mail	立入禁止 **Tachi-iri-kinshi** No entry	満員 **Man'in(g)** Full

1.8 Legal holidays

New Year's Day (January 1) — *Gan-jitsu*

Coming of Age Day (2nd Monday of January) — *Sayjin-no-hi*

National Foundation Day (February 11) — *Ken-koku kinen-no-hi*

Vernal Equinox Day (March 20 or 21) — *Shun-bun-no-hi*

Showa Day (April 29) — *Shohwa-no-hi*

Constitution Day (May 3) — *Kempoh ki-nen-bi*

Greenery Day (May 4) — *Midori-no-hi*

Children's Day (May 5) — *Kodomo-no-hi*

Marine Day (3rd Monday of July) — *Umi-no-hi*

Mountain Day (August 11) — *Yama-no-hi*

Respect for the Aged Day (3rd Monday of September) — *Kayroh-no-hi*

Autumnal Equinox Day (September 23) — *Shoo-bun-no-hi*

Health-Sports Day (2nd Monday of October) — *Tai-iku-no-hi*

Culture Day (November 3)	*Bunka-no-hi*
Thanksgiving Day (November 23)	*Kinroh-kansha-no-hi*
Emperor's Birthday (December 23)	*Tennoh tanjoh-bi*

Only January 1 is an official public holiday during the New Year period, but most banks and businesses remain shut until at least January 3. The period between April 29 and May 5 is known as Golden Week, where four public holidays occur.

The Obon festival, when families return to ancestral homes to venerate the returning spirits of their ancestors, is held in country districts around mid July and in Tokyo in mid August. It should also be noted that Christmas Day is a normal business day.

2. Meet and Greet

Being polite is very important in Japan. When someone does something for you, a simple *dohmo sumimasen* (Thank you for your trouble) is greatly appreciated. On meeting, the Japanese greet each other with a bow from the waist, of varying depth. Non-Japanese need not do so, though people find themselves following this almost unconsciously after a short time. Many Japanese now greet a Westerner with a handshake. Shoes must be taken off when entering private homes, traditional-style restaurants and inns. Physical contact is unavoidable in trains, elevators and other crowded public places. It is polite, however, to maintain a kind of mental privacy. Impatience is rarely shown in public, while displays of anger cause embarrassment and are rarely effective.

2.1 Greetings

Good morning.	*O-ha-yoh (gozai-masu).* おはよう（ございます）。
Hello.	*Kon-nichi-wa.* こんにちは。
Good evening.	*Kom-ban-wa.* こんばんは。
Good afternoon.	*Kon-nichi-wa.* こんにちは。
How are you?	*O-genki des-ka?* お元気ですか。
Fine, thank you, and you?	*Hai, genki des. Anata wa?* はい、元気です。あなたは？
Very well.	*O-kagay-sama day.* おかげさまで。
Not too bad.	*Mah mah des.* まあまあです。

So-so.	*Mah mah.* まあまあ。
I'd better go.	*Jah, shits-ray shimas.* じゃあ、失礼します。

I have to go.
  Someone's waiting
  for me.
	Hito o mata-setay imas no day,
	koray de shits-ray itash-mas.
	人を待たせていますので、
	これで失礼いたします。

Good bye.	*Sayoh-nara.* さよなら。
See you soon.	*Mata ato-day.* またあとで。
Good night.	*Oyasumi na-sai.* お休みなさい。
Good luck.	*Gambat-tay kuda-sai.* がんばってください。
Have fun.	*Tano-shinday kuda-sai.* 楽しんでください。
Have a nice vacation.	*Tanoshee kyooka o.* 楽しい休暇を。
Have a good trip.	*Tanoshee ryokoh o.* 楽しい旅行を。
Thank you, you too.	*Dohmo arigatoh, anata mo.* どうもありがとう。あなたも。
Say hello to...for me.	*... ni yoroshku.* …によろしく。

2.2 Asking a question

Who?	*Daray?* 誰？
Who's that?	*Daray des-ka?* 誰ですか？
What?	*Nani?* 何？
What's there to see here?	*Kono chikaku day nani-ka omoshiroi* *koto ga arimas-ka?* この近くで何か面白いことがありま すか？
What kind of hotel is that?	*Donna hoteru des-ka?* どんなホテルですか？
Where?	*Doko?* どこ？

Where's the bathroom?	*Toiray wa doko ni arimas-ka?* トイレはどこにありますか?
Where are you going?	*Dochira ni ikaremas-ka?* どちらに行かれますか?
Where are you from?	*Doko kara kimashta-ka?* どこから来ましたか?
How?	*Doh?* どう?
How far is that?	*Dono kurai toh-i des-ka?* どのくらい遠いですか?
How long does that take?	*Nan-jikan kakarimas-ka?* 何時間かかりますか?
How long is the trip?	*Dono kurai kakarimas-ka?* どのくらいかかりますか?
How much?	*Ikura des-ka?* いくらですか?
How many?	*Ikuts des-ka?* いくつですか?
How much is this?	*Koray wa ikura des-ka?* これはいくらですか?
Which…?	*Dono...?* どの…?
Which?	*Doray?* どれ?
Which glass is mine?	*Dono koppu ga watashi no des-ka?* どのコップが私のですか?
When?	*Its?* いつ?
When are you leaving?	*Its demas-ka?* いつ出ますか?
Why?	*Dohshtay/nazay?* どうして／なぜ?
Could you help me, please?	*Tetsudat-tay kuda-sai masen-ka?* 手伝ってくださいませんか?
Could you point that out to me?	*Oshie-tay kuda-sai masen-ka?* 教えてくださいませんか?
Could you come with me, please?	*Tsuretay it-tay kuda-sai masen-ka?* 連れていってくださいませんか?

Could you reserve some tickets for me, please?	*Yoyaku shtay itadakemas-ka?* 予約していただけますか?
Do you know...?	*... (o) shit-tay imas-ka?* … (を) 知っていますか?
Do you know of another hotel, please?	*Hoka no hoteru o shohkai shtay kuda-sai.* 他のホテルを紹介してください。
Do you have a...?	*... (ga) arimas-ka?* … (が) ありますか?
Do you have a vegetarian dish, please?	*Bejitarian-ryohri wa arimas-ka?* ベジタリアン料理はありますか?
I'd like...	*... onegai shimas.* …お願いします。
I'd like a kilo of apples, please.	*Ringo o ichi-kiro kuda-sai.* リンゴを一キロ下さい。
Can I take this?	*Kore o mot-tay it-tay mo ee des-ka?* これを持って行ってもいいですか?
Can I smoke here?	*Tabako o sut-tay mo ee des-ka?* タバコを吸ってもいいですか?
Could I ask you something?	*Chotto, keetay mo ee des-ka?* ちょっと、聞いてもいいですか?

2.3 How to reply

Yes, of course.	*Hai, mochiron.* はい、もちろん。
No, I'm sorry.	*Ee-ye, sumimasen.* いいえ、すみません。
Yes, what can I do for you?	*Hai, dohzo.* はい、どうぞ。
Just a moment, please.	*Chotto mat-tay kuda-sai.* ちょっと待ってください。
No, I don't have time now.	*Sumimasen-ga, jikan-ga arimasen.* すみませんが、時間がありません。
No, that's impossible.	*Fukanoh des.* 不可能です。
I think so.	*Soh omo-imas.* そう思います。
No, no one.	*Dare mo imasen.* 誰もいません。

No, nothing.	*Nan demo arimasen.* 何でもありません。
It's okay.	*Die-joh-bu des.* 大丈夫です。
That's right.	*Soray de kekkoh des.* それで結構です。
That's different/wrong.	*Chiga-i-masu.* 違います。
I agree.	*Sansay des.* 賛成です。
I don't agree.	*Sansay deki-masen.* 賛成出来ません。
All right.	*Ee des.* いいです。
Okay.	*Ee des-yo.* いいですよ。
I understand.	*Wakari-mashta.* 分かりました。
Perhaps.	*Tabun.* 多分。
I don't know.	*Wakari-masen./Shiri-masen.* わかりません。／知りません。

2.4 Thank you

Thank you.	*(Dohmo) arigatoh.* （どうも）ありがとう。
You're welcome.	*Doh itashi-mash-tay.* どういたしまして。
Thank you very much.	*Dohmo arigatoh gozai-mas.* どうもありがとうございます。
Very kind of you.	*Go-shinsetsu-ni.* ご親切に。
I enjoyed it very much.	*Hontoh ni tanoshikatta des.* 本当に楽しかったです。
Thank you for your trouble.	*Dohmo arigatoh gozai-mashta.* どうもありがとうございました。
You shouldn't have.	*Sumimasen deshta.* すみませんでした。
That's all right.	*Doh itashi-mashi-tay./Ee des-yo.* どういたしまして。/いいですよ。

2.5 I'm sorry

Excuse me	*Sumimasen* すみません
I'm sorry, I didn't know...	*Mohshi-wakay-arimasen, shiranakatta no-de ...* 申し訳ありません、知らなかったので…
I do apologize.	*Sumimasen deshta.* すみませんでした。
I'm sorry.	*Mohshi-wakay-arimasen.* 申し訳ありません。
I didn't do it on purpose, it was an accident.	*Waza-to yatta wakay de-wa-nai no-de, oyurushi-kuda-sai.* わざとやったわけではないので、お許しください。
It could've happened to anyone.	*Soray wa daray ni demo okori-eru koto des.* それは誰にでも起こりえることです。

2.6 What do you think?

Which do you prefer?	*Dochira ga o-ski des-ka?* どちらがお好きですか?
What do you think?	*Doh omoimas-ka?* どう思いますか?
Don't you like dancing?	*Odoru no ga ki-rai des-ka?* 踊るのが嫌いですか?
I don't mind.	*Nan-demo ee des.* 何でもいいです。
Well done!	*Yokatta!* よかった!
Not bad!	*Waruku-nai des-ne!* 悪くないですね!
Great!	*Subarashee!* すばらしい!
Wonderful food!	*Oi-shee!* おいしい!
It's really nice here!	*Tanoshee des-ne!* 楽しいですねえ!
How nice!	*Steki!* すてき!
How pretty!	*Kiray!* きれい!

How nice for you!	*Ee des-ne!* いいですね！
I'm very happy with...	*... ni manzoku shtay imas* …に満足しています
I'm not very happy with...	*... ni manzoku shtay imasen* …に満足していません
I'm glad...	*... ureshee* …うれしい
I'm having a great time.	*Totemo tanoshinde imas.* とても楽しんでいます。
I'm looking forward to it.	*Soray o tanoshimi ni mat-tay-imas.* それを楽しみに待っています。
That's great!	*Sugoi!* すごい！
What a pity!	*Zannen!* 残念！
That's ridiculous!	*Baka-baka-shee!* ばかばかしい！
What nonsense/How silly!	*Bakara-shee!* ばからしい！
I don't like...	*... wa ki-rai des.* …は嫌いです。
I'm bored to death.	*Unzari da-yo.* うんざりだよ。
I've had enough.	*Moh akita.* もうあきた。
This is no good.	*Damay (da) yo.* だめ（だ）よ。

Hi Yuri! *Kon-nichi wa, Yuri-san.*

Hi Helen. *Kon-nichi wa, Helen-san.* How are things? *O-genki des-ka?*

I'm very well, thank you. *O-kagay-sama day. Arigatoh.*

Hi, pleased to meet you. *Omay ni kakaretay ureshee des.*

Akihiro, this is my friend Helen. *Akihiro-san, kochira wa tomodachi no Helen-san des.*

Where are you from? *O-kuni wa dochira des-ka?*

I'm American. *Amerika-jin des.*

3. Small Talk

3.1 Introductions

May I introduce myself?	*Jiko shohkai shtay mo yoroshee des-ka?* 自己紹介してもよろしいですか？
My name's...	*Watashi-wa... des.* 私は…です。
What's your name?	*O-nama-e wa?* お名前は？
May I introduce...?	*Chotto go-shohkai shimas. ... san des.* ちょっとご紹介します。…さんです。
This is my wife.	*Kochira wa tsuma des.* こちらは妻です。
This is my daughter.	*Kochira wa musumay des.* こちらは娘です。
This is my mother.	*Kochira wa haha des.* こちらは母です。
This is my friend.	*Kochira wa tomodachi des.* こちらは友達です。
This is my husband.	*Kochira wa otto des.* こちらは夫です。
This is my son.	*Kochira wa musko des.* こちらは息子です。
This is my father.	*Kochira wa chichi des.* こちらは父です。

How do you do?	*Hajime-mashtay, dohzo yoroshiku.* 初めまして,どうぞよろしく。
Pleased to meet you.	*O-may ni kakaretay ureshee des.* お目にかかれて嬉しいです。
Where are you from?	*O-kuni wa dochira des-ka?* お国はどちらですか?
I'm from America.	*Amerika kara kimashita des.* アメリカから来ましたです。
I'm from the U.K.	*Igirisu kara kimashita des.* イギリスから来ましたです。
I'm from Australia.	*Ohsutoraria kara kimashita des.* オーストラリアから来ましたです。
I'm from Canada.	*Kanada kara kimashita des.* カナダから来ましたです。
I'm from Singapore.	*Shingapohru kara kimashita des.* シンガポールから来ましたです。
What city do you live in?	*Doko ni o-sumai des-ka?* どこにお住まいですか?
In...	*... ni* …に
It's near...	*Soray wa ... ni chi-kai des* それは…に近いです
Have you been here long?	*Moh nagai no des-ka?* もう長いのですか?
A few days.	*Ni-san nichi des.* 二、三日です。
How long are you staying here?	*Dono gurai koko ni oraremas-ka?* どのぐらいここにおられますか?
We're leaving tomorrow.	*Ashta tachimas.* 明日立ちます。
We're probably leaving in two weeks.	*Ni-shookan-go ni tats tsumori des.* 二週間後に立つつもりです。
Where are you staying?	*Doko ni o-tomari des-ka?* どこにお泊りですか?
In a hotel.	*Hoteru-ni.* ホテルに。
With friends.	*Tomodachi no tokoro-ni.* 友達の所に。
With relatives.	*Shinseki no tokoro-ni.* 親戚の所に。

Are you here on your own?	*Hitori de koraray-mashta-ka?* 一人で来られましたか？
Are you here with your family?	*Gokazoku-to koraray-mashta-ka?* ご家族来られにましたか？
I'm on my own.	*Hitori des.* 一人です。
I'm with my wife.	*Tsuma-to kimashta.* 妻と来ました。
I'm with my husband.	*Otto-to kimashta.* 夫と来ました。
I'm with my family.	*Kazoku-to kimashta.* 家族と来ました。
I'm with a friend/friends.	*Tomodachi-to kimashta.* 友達と来ました。
Are you married?	*Kekkon shtay imas-ka?* 結婚していますか？
Do you have a steady boyfriend/girlfriend?	*Koi-bito wa imas-ka?* 恋人はいますか？
[Female] That's none of your business!	*Kankay-na-i desho!* 関係ないでしょ！
[Male] That's none of your business!	*Kankay-na-i daroh!* 関係ないだろう！
I'm married.	*Kekkon shtay imasu.* 結婚しています。
I'm single.	*Doku-shin des.* 独身です。
I'm separated/divorced.	*Rikon shtay imas.* 離婚しています。
I'm a widow.	*Miboh-jin des.* 未亡人です。
I'm a widower.	*Otoko yamomay des.* 男やもめです。
I live with someone.	*Koibito-to sunday imas.* 恋人と住んでいます。
Do you have any children?	*O-ko-san-wa?* お子さんは？
Do you have any grandchildren?	*O-mago-san-wa?* お孫さんは？
How old are you?	*Shitsuray des-ga, oikuts des-ka?* 失礼ですが、おいくつですか？
How old is your daughter?	*O-joh-san wa ikuts des-ka?* お嬢さんはいくつですか？

How old is your son?	*Musuko-san wa ikuts des-ka?* 息子さんはいくつですか？
I'm/She's/He's...years old.	*...sai des.* …歳です。
What do you do for a living?	*O-shigoto wa nan des-ka?* お仕事は何ですか？
I work in an office.	*Kaisha-in des.* 会社員です。
I'm a student.	*Gaksay des.* 学生です。
I'm unemployed.	*Mushoku des.* 無職です。
I'm retired.	*Tai-shoku shimashta.* 退職しました。
I'm on a disability pension.	*Shoh-gai-sha des.* 障害者です。
I'm a housewife.	*Shufu des.* 主婦です。
Do you like your job?	*O-shigoto wa omoshiroi des-ka?* お仕事は面白いですか？
Most of the time.	*Tai-gai-wa.* たいがいは。
I usually do, but I prefer vacations.	*Mah mah des-ga, yasumi no-hoh-ga omoshiroi des-yo-ne.* まあまあですが、休みの方が面白いで すよね。

3.2 I beg your pardon?

I don't speak any Korean.	*Zen-zen Kankoku-go ha-nasay-masen.* ぜんぜん韓国語話せません。
I speak a little Japanese.	*Skoshi dakay Nihon-go ha-nasay-mas.* 少しだけ日本語話せます。
I'm American.	*Watashi wa Amerika-jin des.* 私はアメリカ人です。
I'm British.	*Watashi wa Igirisu-jin des.* 私はイギリス人です。
I'm Australian.	*Watashi wa Ohsutoraria-jin des.* 私はオーストラリア人です。
I'm Canadian.	*Watashi wa Kanada-jin des.* 私はカナダ人です。
I'm Singaporean.	*Watashi wa Shingapohru-jin des.* 私はシンガポール人です。

Can you speak English?	*Aygo ga hanasay-mas-ka?* 英語が話せますか?
Can you speak Japanese?	*Nihongo ga hanasay mas-ka?* 日本語が話せますか?
Is there anyone who speaks English?	*Koko ni wa Aygo ga hanaseru shito ga imas-ka?* ここには英語が話せる人がいますか?
I beg your pardon?	*Nan-to ossha-i-mashta-ka?* 何とおっしゃいましたか?
I understand.	*Wakari-mashta.* 分かりました。
I don't understand.	*Chotto wakari-masen.* ちょっと分かりません。
Do you understand me?	*Wakarimas-ka?* 分かりますか?
Could you repeat that, please?	*Moh ichido it-tay kuda-sai.* もう一度言ってください。
Could you speak more slowly, please?	*Yuk-kuri hanashtay kuda-sai masen-ka?* ゆっくり話してくださいませんか?
What does that mean?	*Soray wa doh-yoo imi des-ka?* それはどういう意味ですか?
What does that word mean?	*Sono kotoba wa doh-yoo imi des-ka?* その言葉はどういう意味ですか?
Is that similar to/ the same as...?	*Soray wa... to yoo imi des-ka?* それは…という意味ですか?

Could you point that out
  in this phrase book,
  please?
	*Kono hon de oshie-tay kuda-sai
	masen-ka?*
	この本で教えてくださいませんか?

Could you write that down for me, please?	*Soray o kaitay kuda-sai masen-ka?* それを書いてくださいませんか?
One moment, please, I have to look it up.	*Chotto mat-tay kuda-sai, sagashtay mimas.* ちょっと待ってください、捜してみます。
I can't find the word.	*Kotoba ga mitsukari-masen.* 言葉が見つかりません。
How do you say that in Japanese?	*Soray wa Nihon-go nan-to ee-mas-ka?* それは日本語何とう言いますか?

| How do you pronounce that? | *Soray wa doh hatsuon shimas-ka?* それはどう発音しますか? |

3.3 Starting/ending a conversation

Excuse me, could you help me?	*Sumimasen-ga, tasketay kuda-sai.* すみませんが、助けてください。
Yes, what's the problem?	*Doh shimashta-ka?* どうしましたか?
What can I do for you?	*Nani-ka goyoh deshoh-ka?* 何かご用でしょうか?
Sorry, I don't have time now.	*Isogimas no-de, sumimasen.* 急ぎますので、すみません。
Do you have a light?	*Hi o o-mochi des-ka?* 火をお持ちですか?
May I join you?	*Go-issho-shtay mo yoroshee des-ka?* ご一緒してもよろしいですか?
Could you take a picture of me/us?	*Shashin o tot-tay kuda-sai mas-ka?* 写真をとってくださいますか?
Press this button.	*Kono botan o oshtay kuda-sai.* このボタンを押してください。
[Female] Leave me alone!	*Hottoi-tay-yo!* ほっといてよ!
[Male] Leave me alone!	*Hottoi-tay kuray!* ほっといてくれ!
[Female] Get lost!	*At-chi it-tay-yo!* あっちいってよ!
[Male] Get lost!	*At-chi ikay-yo!* あっちいけよ!
[Female] Go away or I'll scream!	*Ikanai-to, sakebu-wa-yo!* 行かないと、叫ぶわよ!
[Male] Go away or I'll yell!	*Ikanai-to, sakebu-zo!* 行かないと、叫ぶぞ!

3.4 A chat about the weather

See also 1.5 The weather

| It's so hot today! | *Kyoh wa atswee des-ne!* 今日は暑いですね! |
| It's so cold today! | *Kyoh wa samui des-ne!* 今日は寒いですね! |

Nice weather, isn't it?	*Ee tenki des-ne?* いい天気ですね?
What a wind!	*Sugoi kazay des-ne!* すごい風ですね!
All that rain!	*Sugoi amay des-ne!* すごい雨ですね!
All that snow!	*Yuki ga sugoi des-ne!* 雪がすごいですね!
All that fog!	*Fukai kiri des-ne!* 深い霧ですね!
Has the weather been like this for long here?	*Koko wa zutto kon-na tenki nan des-ka?* ここはずっとこんな天気なんですか?
Is it always this hot here?	*Kono hen wa its-mo atswee-n des-ka?* この辺はいつも暑いんですか?
Is it always this cold here?	*Kono hen wa its-mo samui-n des-ka?* この辺はいつも寒いんですか?
Is it always this dry here?	*Kono hen wa its-mo amay ga sukunai-n des-ka?* この辺はいつも雨が少ないんですか?
Is it always this wet here?	*Kono hen wa its-mo amay ga oh-ee des-ka?* この辺はいつも雨が多いですか?

3.5 Hobbies

Do you have any hobbies?	*Shoomi-wa?* 趣味は?
I like knitting.	*Amimono ga ski des.* 編みものが好きです。
I like reading.	*Dokusho ga ski des.* 読書が好きです。
I like photography.	*Shashin o toru no-ga ski des.* 写真をとるのが好きです。
I like music.	*Onaku ga ski des.* 音楽が好きです。
I like playing the guitar.	*Gitah o hiku no-ga ski des.* ギターを弾くのが好きです。
I like playing the piano.	*Piano o hiku no-ga ski des.* ピアノを弾くのが好きです。
I like going to the movies.	*Ayga o mi ni iku no-ga ski des.* 映画を見に行くのが好きです。
I like traveling.	*Ryokoh suru no-ga ski des.* 旅行するのが好きです。

I like playing sports.	*Spohts ga ski des.* スポーツが好きです。
I like fishing.	*Tsuri ni iku no-ga ski des.* つりに行くのが好きです。
I like walking.	*Sampo suru no-ga ski des.* 散歩するのが好きです。

3.6 Invitations

Are you doing anything tonight?	*Moh kom-ban no yotay wa kimeta no?* もう今晩の予定は決めたの?
Do you have any plans for today?	*Moh kyoh no kaykaku wa tate-mashta-ka?* もう今日の計画はたてましたか?
Do you have any plans for tonight?	*Moh kom-ban no kaykaku wa tate-mashta-ka?* もう今晩の計画はたてましたか?
Would you like to go out with me?	*Isshoh ni dekake-masen-ka?* 一緒に出かけませんか?
Would you like to go dancing with me?	*Isshoh ni dans o shi-ni iki-masen-ka?* 一緒にダンスをしに行きませんか?
Would you like to have lunch/dinner with me?	*Isshoh ni tabe-masen-ka?* 一緒に食べませんか?
Would you like to come to the beach with me?	*Isshoh ni kaigan e iki-masen-ka?* 一緒に海岸へ行きませんか?
Would you like to come into town with us?	*Isshoh ni machi-e iki-masen-ka?* 一緒に町へ行きませんか?
Would you like to come and meet some friends with us?	*Isshoh ni tomodachi no tokoro ni iki-masen-ka?* 一緒に友達の所に行きませんか?
I don't dance.	*Odori-masen.* 踊りません。
Shall we sit at the bar?	*Bah ni suwari-mashoh-ka?* バーに座りましょうか?
Shall we get something to drink?	*Nani-ka nomi-mashoh-ka?* 何か飲みましょうか?
Shall we go for a walk?	*Sampo ni iki-mashoh-ka?* 散歩に行きましょうか?

Shall we go for a drive?	*Doraibu ni iki-mashoh-ka?* ドライブに行きましょうか？
Good idea.	*Ee des-ne.* いいですね。
No (thank you).	*Ee-ye, kekkoh des.* いいえ、けっこうです。
Maybe later.	*Mata kondo.* また今度。
[Female] I don't feel like it.	*Kyohmi ga nai-wa.* 興味がないわ。
[Male] I don't feel like it.	*Kyohmi ga nai-yo.* 興味がないよ。
[Female] I don't have time.	*Jikan ga nai-wa.* 時間がないわ。
[Male] I don't have time.	*Jikan ga nai-yo.* 時間がないよ。
I already have a date.	*Moh hoka no yakusoku-ga.* もう他の約束が。
I'm not very good at dancing.	*Dans wa heta-des.* ダンスは下手です。
I'm not very good at volleyball.	*Baray-bohru wa heta-des.* バレーボールは下手です。
I can't swim.	*Oyogemasen.* 泳げません。

3.7 Paying a compliment

You look wonderful!	*O-kiray des-ne!* おきれいですね！
I like your car!	*Ee kuruma des-ne!* いい車ですね！
What a sweet child!	*Nantay kawa-ee akachan deshoh!* 何てかわいい赤ちゃんでしょう！
You're a wonderful dancer!	*Dans ga johzu des-ne!* ダンスが上手ですね！
You're a wonderful cook!	*Ryohri ga johzu des-ne!* 料理が上手ですね！
You're a terrific tennis player!	*Tenisu ga johzu des-ne!* テニスが上手ですね！

3.8 Intimate comments/questions

| I like being with you. | *Isshoh ni iru to tanoshee.*
一緒にいると楽しい。 |

[Female] I've missed you so much. — *Tot-tay-mo sabishi-kat-ta-wa.* とっても寂しかったわ。

[Male] I've missed you so much. — *Tot-tay-mo sabishi-kat-ta-yo.* とっても寂しかったよ。

[Female] I dreamt about you. — *Anata no yumay o mita-wa.* あなたの夢をみたわ。

[Male] I dreamt about you. — *Kimi no yumay o mita-yo.* 君の夢をみたよ。

[Male] You're pretty! — *Kiray da-yo!* きれいだよ！

[Female] You're nice. — *Steki-yo.* すてきよ。

[Male] You're nice. — *Steki da-yo.* すてきだよ。

You're sexy. — *Sekshee.* セクシー。

[Female] Look at me. — *Watashi o mitay.* 私を見て。

[Male] Look at me. — *Boku o mitay.* 僕を見て。

You have such beautiful eyes. — *Kiray na hitomi da-ne.* きれいな瞳だね。

[Female] I'm crazy about you. — *Anata ni muchoo na no.* あなたに夢中なの。

[Male] I'm crazy about you. — *Kimi ni muchoo nanda.* 君に夢中なんだ。

I love you. — *Ai-shteru.* 愛してる。

[Female] I love you too. — *Watashi-mo.* 私も。

[Male] I love you too. — *Boku-mo.* 僕も。

[Female] I don't feel as strongly about you. — *Watashi no kimochi wa chigau no.* 私の気持ちは違うの。

[Male] I don't feel as strongly about you. — *Boku no kimochi wa chigaun-da.* 僕の気持ちは違うんだ。

I already have a boyfriend/girlfriend. — *Moh koibito ga iru.* もう恋人がいる。

I'm not ready for that. — *Moh skoshi mat-tay.* もう少し待って。

[Female] This is going too fast for me. — *Sugoku haya-sugiru no.* すごく早過ぎるの。

[Male] This is going too fast for me.	*Sugoku haya-sugiru-yo.* すごく早過ぎるよ。
[Female] Take your hands off me.	*Sawara-nai-day.* 触らないで。
Will you stay with me tonight?	*Konya issoh ni tomara-nai?* 今夜一緒に泊まらない？
I'd like to go to bed with you.	*Ai-shi-tai.* 愛したい。
Only if we use a condom.	*Kondohm o tsukat-tay kureru-nara.* コンドームを使ってくれるなら。
We have to be careful about AIDS.	*Ayzu no koto mo aru kara.* エイズのこともあるから。
[Female] That's what they all say.	*Otokot-tay mina soh yoo no-ne.* 男って皆そういうのね。
[Female] We shouldn't take any risks.	*Kiken wa sakay mashoh-yo.* 危険は避けましょうよ。
[Male] We shouldn't take any risks.	*Kiken wa sakay-yoh-yo.* 危険は避けようよ。
Do you have a condom?	*Kondohm motteru?* コンドームもってる？
[Female] No? In that case we won't do it.	*Sore-nara, yamemashoh.* それなら、やめましょう。
[Male] No? In that case we won't do it.	*Sore-nara, yameyoh.* それなら、やめよう。

3.9 Congratulations and condolences

| Happy birthday/many happy returns. | *O-tanjoh-bi omedetoh (gozai-mas).* お誕生日おめでとう(ございます)。 |
| Please accept my condolences. | *Kokoro-kara o-kuyami mohshi-agemas.* 心からお悔やみ申し上げます。 |

3.10 Arrangements

| When will I see you again? | *Kondo its aemas-ka?* 今度いつ会えますか？ |

Are you free over the weekend?	*Kono shoomats o-hima des-ka?* この週末おひまですか?
What shall we do?	*Nani-ka kay-kaku shimashoh-ka?* 何か計画しましょうか?
Where shall we meet?	*Doko de aimashoh-ka?* どこで会いましょうか?
Will you pick me/us up?	*Kuruma de hirot-tay kuremas-ka?* 車で拾ってくれますか?
Shall I pick you up?	*Kuruma de hiroi mashoh-ka?* 車で拾いましょうか?
I have to be home by...	*...ji-made ni kaera-nai-to* …時までに帰らないと
I don't want to see you anymore.	*Moh aitaku-nai.* もう会いたくない。

3.11 Being the host(ess)

See also 4 Eating out

Can I offer you a drink?	*Nani-ka o-nomi-ni-nari-masen-ka?* 何かお飲みになりませんか?
What would you like to drink?	*Nani o o-nomi ni narimas-ka?* 何をお飲みになりますか?
Would you like a cigarette?	*Tabako wa ikaga des-ka?* タバコはいかがですか?
Would you like a cigar?	*Hamaki wa ikaga des-ka?* 葉巻はいかがですか?
Something (a drink that is) non-alcoholic, please.	*Arukohru-nashi no nomimono o kuda-sai.* アルコールなしの飲み物をください。
I don't smoke.	*Tabako wa swee-masen.* たばこは吸いません。

3.12 Saying good-bye

| Can I take you home? | *Okut-tay it-tay mo ee des-ka?* 送っていってもいいですか? |

Can I write?	*Tegami o kaitay mo ee des-ka?* 手紙を書いてもいいですか?
Can I email you?	*May-ru o shtay mo ee des-ka?* メールをしてもいいですか?
Can I call you?	*Denwa o kaketay mo ee des-ka?* 電話をかけてもいいですか?
Will you write to me?	*Tegami o kuremas-ka?* 手紙をくれますか?
Will you call me?	*Denwa o kuremas-ka?* 電話をくれますか?
Can I have your address?	*Anata no joosho o oshie-tay kuremas-ka?* あなたの住所を教えてくれますか?
Can I have your phone number?	*Anata no denwa bangoh o oshie-tay kuremas-ka?* あなたの電話番号を教えてくれますか?
May I know your email address?	*May-ru adores o oshie-tay kuremas-ka?* メールアドレスを教えてくれますか?
Thanks for everything.	*Iro-iro arigatoh gozai-mashta.* いろいろありがとうございました。
It was very nice.	*Totemo tanoshi-katta des.* とても楽しかったです。
Say hello to...	*... san ni yoroshku* …さんによろしく
All the best.	*Genki de-ne.* 元気でね。
When will you be back?	*Its kaeru?* いつ帰る?
[Female] I'll be waiting for you.	*May-tayru-wa.* 待ってるわ。
[Male] I'll be waiting for you.	*May-tayru-yo.* 待ってるよ。
I'd like to see you again.	*Mata ai-tai-wa.* また会いたいわ。
This is our address.	*Watashi-tachi no joosho des.* 私たちの住所です。
If you're ever in the U.S., you'd be more than welcome.	*Its-demo Amerika ni irashtara dohzo.* いつでもアメリカ にいらしたらどうぞ。

4. Eating out

Large cities like Tokyo offer a vast selection of restaurants with food from all over the world. All department stores and shopping malls have two or more restaurant floors, with individual restaurants serving many varieties of Japanese, Chinese and Western food. Back alleys and side streets usually have a variety of small restaurants to choose from. Food selection is very easy in Japan because many restaurants have models of the dishes offered in their window displays or menus with photos of the dishes. Children are usually welcome at local restaurants and those in shopping centers and train stations, but not at exclusive, upscale restaurants and bars. Traditional restaurants with *tatami* (straw-matted) seating areas are a benefit for those with babies.

At the restaurant

Can you help me make a reservation for two, please?	*Ftari-bun no yoyaku o shi-tai no des-ga?* 二人分の予約をしたいのですが?
I'd like a table please.	*Tehburu-seki o yoyaku shi-tai no des-ga.* テーブル席を予約したいのですが。
I'd like a table for two, please.	*Ftari-bun no tehburu o onegai shimas.* 二人分のテーブルをお願いします。
We've reserved.	*Yoyaku shimashta.* 予約しました。
We haven't reserved.	*Yoyaku shtay imasen.* 予約していません。
What time does the restaurant open?	*Restoran wa nan-ji-kara des-ka?* レストランは何時からですか?

| What time does the restaurant close? | *Restoran wa nan-ji maday des-ka?*
レストランは何時までですか? |

ご予約ですか?	Do you have a reservation?
お名前は?	What name, please?
喫煙席と禁煙席、どちらになさいますか?	Smoking or non-smoking?
喫煙席をお願いします。	Smoking, please.
禁煙席をお願いします。	Non-smoking, please.
こちらへ。	This way, please.
このテーブルは予約済みです。	This table is reserved.
15分お待ちいただくとテーブルが空きます。	We'll have a table free in 15 minutes.
お待ちになりますか?	Would you like to wait?

Can we wait for a table?	*Tehburu ga aku-made machi-tai no des-ga?* テーブルが空くまで待ちたいのですが?
Do we have to wait long?	*Nagaku machimas-ka?* 長く待ちますか?
How long is the wait?	*Dono-kurai machimas-ka?* どのくらい待ちますか?
Is this seat taken?	*Kono seki aitay imas-ka?* この席、空いてますか?
Could we sit here?	*Koko ni suwat-tay mo ee des-ka?* ここに座ってもいいですか?
Could we sit there?	*Asoko ni suwat-tay mo ee des-ka?* あそこに座ってもいいですか?
Can we sit by the window?	*Mado-giwa ni suwat-tay mo ee des-ka?* 窓ぎわに座ってもいいですか?
Can we eat outside?	*Soto demo taberaremas-ka?* 外でも食べられますか?
Do you have another chair for us?	*Isu moh hitots arimas-ka?* 椅子もう一つありますか?
Do you have a child's chair?	*Kodomo-yoh no isu ga arimas-ka?* 子供用の椅子がありますか?

Could you warm up this bottle/jar for me?	*Sumimasen-ga, kono (ho-nyoo) bin o atatametay kuremas-ka?* すみませんが、この（ほ乳）びんを温めてくれますか？
Not too hot, please.	*Atsu-sugi-nai yoh ni onegai shimasu.* 熱過ぎないようにお願いします。
Is there somewhere I can change the baby's diaper?	*Bebee-room wa arimas-ka?* ベビールームはありますか？
Where are the restrooms?	*Toire wa doko des-ka?* トイレはどこですか？

4.2 Ordering

We'd like something to eat.	*Nani-ka tabe-tai-n des-ga.* 何か食べたいんですが。
We'd like a drink.	*Nani-ka nomi-tai-n des-ga.* 何か飲みたいんですが。
Could I have a quick meal?	*Nani-ka hayaku dekiru shina wa arimas-ka?* 何か早く出来る品はありますか？
We don't have much time.	*Isoi-de iru no des-ga.* 急いでいるのですが。
We'd like to have a drink first.	*Mazu nani-ka nomi-tai-n des-ga.* 先ず何か飲みたいんですが。
Do you have an English menu?	*Aygo no menyoo wa arimas-ka?* 英語のメニューはありますか？
Do you have a dish of the day?	*Kyoh no o-susume wa arimas-ka?* 今日のおすすめはありますか？
We haven't made a choice yet.	*Mada kimari-masen.* まだ決りません。
What do you recommend?	*O-susume wa nan des-ka?* おすすめは何ですか？
What are the specials?	*O-susume-ryohri wa nan des-ka?* おすすめ料理は何ですか？
I don't like...	*... wa ski ja nai-n des* …は好きじゃないんです

I like fish.	*Sakana ga ski des.* 魚が好きです。
I like meat.	*Niku ga ski des.* 肉が好きです。
Can we order the chef's menu, please?	*Omakase onegai shimas.* おまかせお願いします。
Mixed sushi, please.	*Sushi moriawase onegai shimas.* すし盛り合わせお願いします。
Mixed sashimi, please.	*Sashimi moriawase onegai shimas.* 刺身盛り合わせお願いします。
What's this?	*Koray wa nan des-ka?* これは何ですか?
Does it have...in it?	*... ga hait-tay imas-ka?* …が入っていますか?
Is this a hot dish?	*Kono ryohri wa atata-kai des-ka?* この料理は温かいですか?
Is this a cold dish?	*Kono ryohri wa tsume-tai des-ka?* この料理は冷たいですか?
Is this sweet?	*Kono ryohri wa ama-i des-ka?* この料理は甘いですか?
Is this spicy?	*Kono ryohri wa kara-i des-ka?* この料理は辛いですか?
Do you have anything else, please?	*Hoka ni nani-ka arimas-ka?* 他に何かありますか?
I'm on a salt-free diet.	*Shio-nuki de onegai shimas.* 塩ぬきでお願いします。
I don't eat pork.	*Buta-niku wa taberare-masen.* 豚肉は食べられません。
I don't eat sugar.	*Satoh wa taberare-masen.* 砂糖は食べられません。
I don't eat fatty food.	*Aburap-poy ryohri wa taberare-masen.* 油っぽい料理は食べられません。
I don't eat spicy food.	*(Karai) spais wa taberare-masen.* (辛い) スパイスは食べられません。
I'll/we'll have what those people are having.	*Ano-hito-to onaji ryohri o, onegai shimas.* あの人と同じ料理を、お願いします。
I'd like X.	*X onegai shimas.* X お願いします。

Do you have a knife and fork?	*Naif to fohk arimas-ka?* ナイフとフォークありますか?
A little more rice please.	*Gohan moh skoshi onegai shimas.* ご飯もう少しお願いします。
Another glass of water please.	*Mizu moh ip-pai onegai shimas.* 水もう一杯お願いします。
A glass of beer please.	*Biru ip-pai onegai shimas.* ビル一杯お願いします。
A glass of wine please.	*Wain ip-pai onegai shimas.* ワイン一杯お願いします。
One more please.	*Moh hitots onegai shimas.* もう一つお願いします。
Do you have salt and pepper?	*Shio to koshoh arimas-ka?* 塩と胡椒ありますか?
Do you have a napkin?	*Napukin arimas-ka?* ナプキンありますか?
Do you have a spoon?	*Supoon arimas-ka?* スプーンありますか?
Do you have an ashtray?	*Hai-zara arimas-ka?* 灰皿ありますか?
Do you have any matches?	*Matchi arimas-ka?* マッチありますか?
Do you have any toothpicks?	*Tsuma-yohji arimas-ka?* つまようじありますか?
Can I have a glass of water, please?	*Mizu ip-pai onegai shimas.* 水一杯お願いします。
Do you have a straw?	*Stroh arimas-ka?* ストローありますか?
Let's eat! Bon appetit!	*Itadakimas!* いただきます!
Cheers!	*Kam-pai!* 乾杯!
The next round's on me.	*Kondo wa watashi ga ogorimas.* 今度は私がおごります。
It's on me today. (It's my treat.)	*Kyoh wa watashi no ogori des.* 今日は私のおごりです。
Thank you for the meal.	*Gochisoh sama deshta.* ごちそうさまでした。

4.3 The bill

See also 8.2 Settling the bill

How much is this dish?   *Kono ryohri wa ikura des-ka?*
この料理はいくらですか?

Could I have the
bill, please?   *O-kanjoh onegai shimas.*
お勘定、お願いします。

All together.   *Issho-de.* 一緒で。

Separate checks, please.   *Bets-bets de onegai shimas.*
別々でお願いします。

Could we have the
menu again, please?   *Moh ik-kai menyoo o misetay kuda-sai.*
もう一回メニューを見せてください。

No, let's split the bill.   *Ee-ye, warikan ni shimashoh.*
いいえ、割り勘にしましょう。

The...is not on the bill.   *... ga hait-tay imasen.*
…が入っていません。

4.4 Complaints

It's taking a very
long time.   *Zuibun jikan ga kakat-tay imas-ne.*
ずいぶん時間がかかっていますね。

We've been here an
hour already.   *Moh ichi-jikan mo mat-tay imas.*
もう一時間も待っています。

This must be a mistake.   *Koray wa machigai deshoh.*
これは間違いでしょう。

This is not what I ordered.   *Koray wa choomon shtay-masen.*
これは注文してません。

I ordered...   *... o choomon shimashta.*
…を注文しました。

There's a dish missing.   *Ryohri ga ip-pin tari-masen.*
料理が一品足りません。

This is broken.   *Kore wa kowarete-imas.*
これは壊れています。

This is not clean.   *Chotto, koray kita-nai-n des-ga.*
ちょっと、これ汚いんですが。

The food's cold.	*Ryohri ga tsume-tai-n des-ga.* 料理が冷たいんですが。
The food is not fresh.	*Koray wa shinsen ja nai des.* これは新鮮じゃないです。
The food is too salty.	*Koray wa shio kara-i des.* これは塩辛いです。
The food is too sweet.	*Koray wa ama-sugimas.* これは甘過ぎます。
The food is too spicy.	*Koray wa kara-sugimas.* これは辛過ぎます。
The meat's not cooked enough.	*Niku ga yaketay-masen.* 肉が焼けてません。
The meat is overdone.	*Niku ga yaki-sugi des.* 肉が焼き過ぎです。
The meat is tough.	*Niku ga ka-tai des.* 肉が堅いです。
The meat is spoiled.	*Niku ga kusat-tay imas.* 肉がくさっています。
Could I have something else instead of this?	*Kawari no shina o morae-masen-ka?* 代わりの品をもらえませんか?
The bill/this amount is not right.	*Kanjoh ga aimasen.* 勘定が合いません。
We didn't have this.	*Koray wa tabetay-masen.* これは食べてません。
There's no toilet paper in the restroom.	*Toiretto-pehpah ga nai des.* トイレットペーパーがないです。
Will you get the manager, please?	*Sekinin-sha o yonday kuda-sai.* 責任者を呼んでください。

4.5 Paying a compliment

| That was a wonderful meal. | *Totemo oishikatta-des.*
とてもおいしかったです。 |
| The food was excellent. | *Gochisoh sama deshta.*
ごちそうさまでした。 |

| The...in particular was delicious. | *Toku ni ... ga totemo oishikatta-des.*
特に…がとてもおいしかったです。 |

4.6 The menu

The following are some popular Japanese dishes:

しゃぶしゃぶ　　*Shabu shabu*
Thin strips of pork or beef and various vegetables cooked at your table in a boiling pot of clear broth and eaten with dipping sauces.

焼き鳥　　*Yakitori*
Marinated chicken skewers, cooked over a brazier.

味噌汁　　*Misoshiru*
Soup made from miso (fermented soy bean paste) with tofu and small mushrooms.

うどん、そば　　*Udon, soba*
Thick white and thin brown noodles respectively. Served either cold with dipping sauces (good in summer) or warm in a soup, with various toppings.

茶わんむし　　*Chawan-mushi*
Fish and vegetables steamed in an egg custard in a small teacup.

豚カツ　　*Tonkatsu*
Pork cutlets fried in breadcrumbs and served with a thick brown sauce.

親子どんぶり　　*Oyako domburi*
Chicken and egg served on rice. A popular lunch dish.

カレーライス　　*Karay raisu*
The Japanese version of curry and rice. Usually beef, chicken, or pork pieces in a curry sauce.

お好み焼き　　*Okonomiyaki*
A Japanese stuffed pancake containing a variety of ingredients such as vegetables, meat and seafood. *Okonomiyaki* originally came from the Hiroshima area of Japan, but is widely available throughout the country. Toppings and batters vary according to region.

居酒屋 *Izakaya*

Pub or bar food—many small dishes like tapas prepared behind a bar and served with drinks. Usually includes cold appetizers (like sashimi), soups and hot grilled dishes, including chicken, beef and vegetables.

おにぎり *Onigiri*

Also known as *omusubi* (おむすび) or rice ball, *onigiri* is a Japanese food made from white rice formed into triangular or oval shapes and often wrapped in seaweed. Traditionally, an *onigiri* is filled with pickled plum, salted salmon, bonito flakes, kelp, salted roe, or any other salty or sour ingredient as a natural preservative. Most convenience stores stock *onigiri* with various fillings and flavors.

オムライス *Omurice*

Chicken ketchup rice wrapped in a thin sheet of fried egg and usually topped with ketchup. This dish is popular with children and is often featured on kids' menus.

焼きそば *Yakisoba*

Literally means 'fried noodles'. It has ramen-style noodles, bite-sized pork, cabbage, onions and carrots flavored with brown *yakisoba* sauce. It is often sold at festivals and street stalls in Japan.

焼き肉 *Yakiniku*

Means 'grilled meat' and is similar to Korean barbecue. Today, it commonly refers to a Japanese style of cooking bite-sized pieces of beef or pork on griddles over a wood charcoal (*sumibi* 炭火) or gas flame.

寿司 *Sushi*

Raw or cooked fish and seafood, over rice seasoned with rice vinegar, wine and sugar. Sushi is the most famous Japanese dish outside of Japan, and one of the most popular dishes among the Japanese themselves.

ラーメン *Ramen*

Thin wheat noodles with a soup broth usually made from pork, chicken or fish and flavoured with soy sauce, salt or miso. Nearly every region of Japan has its own version of this classic.

5. Getting Around

5.1 Asking directions

Excuse me, could I ask you something?	*Chotto, sumimasen.* ちょっと、すみません。
I've lost my way.	*Michi ni mayot-tay shimatta-n-des-ga.* 道に迷ってしまったんですが。
Is there a(n) X around here?	*Kono hen ni X ga arimas-ka?* この辺にXがありますか?
Is this the way to Harajuku station?	*Kono michi wa Harajuku eki e ikimas-ka?* この道は原宿駅へ行きますか?
Could you tell me how to get to Harajuku station?	*Harajuku eki e doh iku-ka oshie-tay kuda-sai-masen-ka?* 原宿駅へどう行くか教えてくださいませんか?
What's the quickest way to Narita Airport?	*Narita kookoh e no ichiban chika-michi wa dore des-ka?* 成田空港への一番近道はどれですか?
How many kilometers to Meiji Shrine?	*Meiji jinja maday nankiro-gurai des-ka?* 明治神社まで何キロぐらいですか?
Could you point it out on the map?	*Kono chizu de oshie-tay morae-masen-ka?* この地図で教えてもらえませんか?

straight ahead	traffic light	overpass	left
mas-sugu	*shingoh*	*kohka-kyo*	*hidari ni*
真っ直ぐ	信号	高架橋	左に
intersection	tunnel	bridge	right
kohsaten	*ton'neru*	*hashi*	*migi ni*
交差点	トンネル	橋	右に
street	at the corner	arrow	cross
michi	*magari-kado de*	*yajirushi*	*watat-tay*
道	曲がり角で	矢印	渡って
main road	river	building	
dori	*kawa*	*tatemono/biru*	
取り	川	建物／ビル	

5.2 The car

See the diagram on page 61

An international driving license is required to drive in Japan. Traffic drives on the left. The speed limit varies but is usually around 40 kph in urban areas and 80 kph on highways; it is 100 kph on expressways. Driving can be complicated because, on some highways, signs are only written in Japanese characters, thus it might be good to rent an English GPS device or use Google Maps to find your way around. Expressways are expensive due to the many toll booths and private toll roads, especially in scenic areas.

GPS	hybrid car
jee-pee-esu	*hai-burid-do-kah/-sha*
GPS(ジーピーエス)	ハイブリッドカー／車
green car	electric car
gureen-kah/eko-kah	*denki jidohsha*
グリーンカー／エコカー	電気自動車

The parts of a car

(The numbers below refer to the diagram)

1	battery	*batteree*	バッテリー
2	rear light	*bakku-rait*	バック・ライト
3	rear-view mirror	*bakku-mirah*	バック・ミラー
	backup light	*bakku-upp-rait*	バックアップ・ライト
4	gas tank	*nenryoh-tanku*	燃料タンク／ガソリン・タンク
		gasorin-tanku	
5	spark plugs	*spahk puragu*	スパーク・プラグ
	fuel filter/pump	*nenryoh firutah/pomp*	燃料フィルター／ ポンプ
6	side mirror	*saido-mirah*	サイド・ミラー
7	trunk	*toranku*	トランク
8	headlight	*heddo-rait*	ヘッド・ライト
9	air filter	*e-a firutah*	エア・フィルター
10	door	*do-a*	ドア
11	radiator	*raji-aytah*	ラジエーター
12	brake disc	*burayki-disk*	ブレーキ・ディスク
13	indicator	*hohkoh-shijiki*	方向指示器
14	windshield wiper	*wai-pah*	ワイパー
15	seat belt	*sheet-beruto*	シートベルト
16	wheel	*tai-ya*	タイヤ
17	spare wheel	*supe-a tai-ya*	スペア・タイヤ

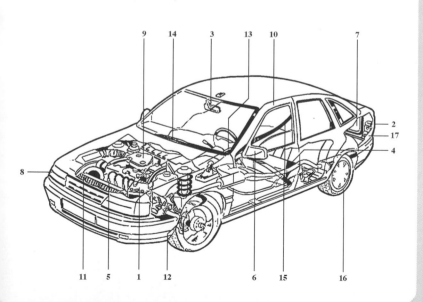

5.3 The gas station

How many kilometers to the next gas station, please?	*Tsugi no gasorin-sutando maday nan-kiro gurai des-ka?* 次のガソリン・スタンドまで何キロぐらいですか?
I would like 50 liters of super gasoline, please.	*Hai-oku o go-joo rit-toru onegai shimas.* ハイオクを50リットルお願いします。
I would like 50 liters of unleaded gasoline, please.	*Mu-en o go-joo rit-toru onegai shimas.* 無鉛を50リットルお願いします。
I would like 50 liters of diesel, please.	*Dee-zerun o go-joo rit-toru onegai shimas.* ディーゼルを50リットルお願いします。
I would like 50 liters of regular gasoline, please.	*Regurah o go-joo rit-toru onegai shimas.* レギュラーを50リットルお願いします。
I would like...yen's worth of gasoline, please.	*... en bun dakay gasorin onegai shimas.* …円分だけガソリンお願いします。
Full tank, please.	*Mantan onegai shimas.* 満タンお願いします。
Could you check the oil level, please?	*Oyru o tenken shtay kuda-sai.* オイルを点検してください。
Could you check the tire pressure, please?	*Tai-ya no kooki-ats o tenken shtay kuda-sai.* タイヤの空気圧を点検してください。
Could you change the oil, please?	*Oyru o ka-etay kuremas-ka?* オイルを替えてくれますか?
Could you clean the windshield, please?	*Fronto garas o fu-itay kuremas-ka?* フロントガラスをふいてくれますか?
Could you wash the car, please?	*Sensha onegai shimas.* 洗車お願いします。

5.4 Breakdowns and repairs

I'm having car trouble. Could you help me, please?	*Kuruma ga koshoh shimashta.* *Tetsu-dat-tay kuda-sai masen-ka?* 車が故障しました。手伝ってくださいませんか?

I've run out of gas.	*Gasorin ga nai-n des-ga.* ガソリンがないんですが。
I've locked the keys in the car.	*Kagi o kuruma no naka ni wasuretay shimai-mashta.* 鍵を車の中に忘れてしまいました。
The engine won't start.	*Enjin ga kakari-masen.* エンジンがかかりません。
Could you call a garage for me, please?	*Shoori-ya o yonday kure-masen-ka?* 修理屋を呼んでくれませんか?
Could you give me a lift to X?	*X maday nosetay kuda-sai masen-ka?* Xまで乗せてくださいませんか?
Could you give me a lift to a garage?	*Shoori-ya maday nosetay kuda-sai masen-ka?* 修理屋まで乗せてくださいませんか?
Could you give me a lift into town?	*Machi maday nosetay kuda-sai masen-ka?* 町まで乗せてくださいませんか?
Can we take my bicycle?	*Jitensha mo mot-tay ikemas-ka?* 自転車も持って行けますか?
Can we take my scooter?	*Skootah mo mot-tay ikemas-ka?* スクーターも持って行けますか?
Could you tow the car to a garage?	*Shoori-ya maday kuruma o hakonday kuda-sai masen-ka?* 修理屋まで車を運んでくださいませんか?
There's probably something wrong with... (See 5.2 and 5.6)	*... ga warui-n des-ga.* …が悪いんですが。
Can you fix it?	*Shoori deki-mas-ka?* 修理できますか?
Could you fix my tire?	*Tai-ya o shoori shtay kuda-sai.* タイヤを修理してください。
Could you change this tire?	*Kono tai-ya o kohkan shtay kuda-sai.* このタイヤを交換してください。

この自動車の部品はありません。
  I don't have parts for your car.
この自転車の部品はありません。
  I don't have parts for your car/bicycle.
部品はどこか他へ取りに行かなければなりません。
  I have to get the parts from somewhere else.
部品を注文しなければなりません。 I have to order the parts.
半日かかります。 That will take half a day.
一日かかります。 That will take a day.
二、三日かかります。 That will take a few days.
一週間かかります。 That will take a week.
全損です。 Your car is a write-off.
全然修理出来ません。 It can't be repaired.
…時に自動車を取りに来れます。 The car will be ready at
  ...o'clock.
…時にオートバイを取りに来れます。 The motorcycle will be
  ready at ...o'clock.
…時に原付バイクを取りに来れます。 The moped will be ready
  at ...o'clock.
…時に自転車を取りに来れます。 The bicycle will be ready at
  ...o'clock.

Can you fix it so it'll get me to...?	*... e ikeru maday no shoori o onegai deki-mas-ka?* …へ行けるまでの修理をお願いできますか?
Which garage can help me?	*Dono shoori-ya de (shoori) dekimas-ka?* どの修理屋で(修理)出来ますか?
When will my car/ bicycle be ready?	*Its tori ni koremas-ka?* いつ取りに来れますか?
Can I wait for it here?	*Koko de matemas-ka?* ここで待てますか?
How much will it cost?	*Ikura kakarimas-ka?* いくらかかりますか?
Could you itemize the bill?	*Kanjoh no maysai o kai-tay kuda-sai.* 勘定の明細を書いてください。

| Can I have a receipt for the insurance? | *Hoken saykyoo-yoh no ryohshoo-sho o kuda-sai.*
保険請求用の領収書をください。 |

5.5 Renting a vehicle

I'd like to rent a...	*... o kari-tai-n des-ga.* …を借りたいんですが。
Here is my driver's license.	*Kore ga unten-menkyo-shoh des.* これが運転免許証です。
Do I need a (special) licence for that?	*(tokubets na) Unten-menkyo-shoh ga irimas-ka?* (特別な)運転免許証がいりますか?
Could I have a receipt for the deposit?	*Hoshoh-kin no ryoh-shoo-sho onegai shimas.* 保証金の領収書お願いします。
How much is the surcharge per kilometer?	*Ichi-kiro ni tsuki tsweeka-ryohkin wa ikura des-ka?* 1キロにつき追加料金はいくらですか?
Does that include gas?	*Gasorin-dai wa hai-tay imas-ka?* ガソリン代は入っていますか?
Does that include insurance?	*Hoken wa fuku-maretay imas-ka?* 保険は含まれていますか?
What time can I pick it up tomorrow?	*Ashta nan-ji ni tori ni koremas-ka?* 明日何時に取りにこれますか?
When does (the car) have to be back?	*Nan-ji maday ni modose-ba ee des-ka?* 何時までに戻せばいいですか?
Where's the gas tank?	*Tank wa doko des-ka?* タンクはどこですか?
What sort of fuel does it take?	*Dono gasorin o tsukae-ba ee des-ka?* どのガソリンを使えばいいですか?
Can I set the GPS to English?	*Aygo de jee-pee-esu o setto dekimas-ka?* 英語でGPSをセットできますか?
Will it be able to find ...?	*(...) ni tsuku koto wa dekisoh des-ka?* (…)に着くことはできそうですか?

5.6 Bicycles/mopeds

See the diagram on page 67

The bicycle is used by commuters to get to stations and by house-wives for local shopping. Most cyclists use footpaths; cycle paths are rare. Bicycles can be hired by the hour or day at most tourist centers, usually near the main station, and with the cycle maps provided, allow for convenient sightseeing.

I'd like to rent a bicycle for one day.	*Ichi-nichi kari-tai-n des-ga.*	一日借りたいんですが。
I'd like to rent a bicycle for two days.	*Futsuka kari-tai-n des-ga.*	二日借りたいんですが。
How much per day?	*Ichi-nichi ikura des-ka?*	一日いくらですか？
How much per week?	*Is-shookan ikura des-ka?*	一週間いくらですか？
How much is the deposit?	*Hoshoh-kin wa ikura des-ka?*	保証金はいくらですか？

The parts of a bicycle

(Most parts sound like the words in English, so if in doubt, pronounce the English word the Japanese way.)

	generator	*hatsu-denki*	発電器
	frame	*fraym*	フレーム
	chain guard	*chayn kabah*	チェーン・カバー
	child's seat	*chai-rudo-sheeto*	チャイルドシート
	rim	*rimu*	リム
1	rear wheel	*koh-rin*	後輪
2	gear change	*hen-soku-ki*	変速機
3	chain	*chayn*	チェーン
4	headlight	*heddo raito*	ヘッドライト
	bulb	*den-kyoo*	電球
5	pump	*kooki-iray*	空気入れ
6	reflector	*hansha-kyoh*	反射鏡

7	brake shoe	*burayki brok*	ブレーキ・ブロック
8	brake cable	*burayki kayburu*	ブレーキ・ケーブル
9	carrier straps	*nidai-rohp*	荷台ロープ
10	spoke	*spohk*	スポーク
11	mudguard	*doro-yokay*	泥よけ
12	handlebar	*handoru*	ハンドル
13	toe clip	*toh-kuripp*	トウクリップ
14	drum brake	*doram-burayki*	ドラム・ブレーキ
15	valve	*choob*	チューブ
16	valve tube	*tai-ya barubu*	タイヤバルブ
17	gear cable	*gee-a kayburu*	ギア・ケーブル
18	front wheel	*zen-rin*	前輪
19	seat	*sadoru*	サドル

electric bicycle
dendo jitensha
電動自転車

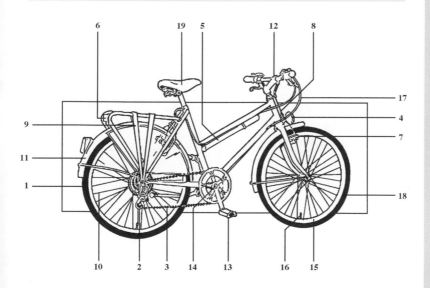

67

5.7 Hitchhiking

Hitchhiking is rare in Japan, but foreign tourists sometimes do it to get from city to city. This requires advance planning and in-depth knowledge of the route, and is best for travelers who have lots of time to spare. The best places to get a ride from are the service areas or parking areas on toll expressways that connect cities, outside an interchange, a gas station on the way to the expressway, or outside a convenience store. It's recommended to produce a sign with your destination (or the next service area so the driver does not have to drive you all the way) written in Japanese, as well as a declaration of your proficiency in the language. Travelers with some knowledge of Japanese will have a higher chance of success. Bring small souvenirs from your home country (*okaeshi*) to thank your hosts for the ride.

Where are you heading?	*Doko e ikimas-ka?* どこへ行きますか?
Can I come along?	*Nosetay kuda-sai mas-ka?* 乗せてくださいますか?
Can my friend come too?	*Tomodachi mo nosetay kuda-sai mas-ka?* 友達も乗せてくださいますか?
I speak Japanese.	*Nihon-go ga dekimasu.* 日本語ができます。
I'm trying to get to...	*... ni iki-tai-n des-ga.* …に行きたいんですが。
Is that on the way to...?	*... to onaji hoh-gaku des-ka?* …と同じ方角ですか?
Could you drop me off here?	*Koko de oroshtay kuda-sai.* ここで降ろしてください。
Could you drop me off at the next exit?	*Tsugi no deguchi de oroshtay kuda-sai.* 次の出口で降ろしてください。
Could you drop me off in the center?	*Chooshin de oroshtay kuda-sai.* 中心で降ろしてください。
Could you drop me off at the next intersection?	*Tsugi no kohsaten de oroshtay kuda-sai.* 次の交差点で降ろしてください。

Could you drop me off at the next service station?	*Tsugi no saabisu eria (esu-ay) de oroshtay kuda-sai.* 次のサービスエリア(ＳＡ)で降ろしてください。
Could you stop here, please?	*Koko de tometay kuda-sai.* ここで止めてください。
I'd like to get out here.	*Koko de oroshtay kuda-sai.* ここで降ろしてください。
Thanks for the lift.	*Arigatoh gozai-mashta.* ありがとうございました。
I don't know if you'll like it, but here is a small gift.	*O-suki ka doh-ka wakari-masen ga doh-zo.* お好きかどうかわかりませんがどうぞ。

6. Arrival and Departure

6.1 General

Where does this train go to?	*Kono densha wa doko e ikimas-ka?* この電車はどこへ行きますか?
Does this boat go to Hokkaido?	*Kono funay wa Hokkaido e ikimas-ka?* この船は北海道へ行きますか?
Can I take this bus to the Meiji Shrine?	*Kono bas wa Meiji jinja e ikimas-ka?* このバスは明治神社へ行きますか?
Does this train stop at Tokyo?	*Kono densha wa Tokyo ni tomarimas-ka?* この電車は東京に止まりますか?
Are these priority seats?	*Kono seki wa yoo-sen seki des-ka?* この席は優先席ですか?
Is this seat free?	*Kono seki wa aitay imas-ka?* この席は空いていますか?
Is this seat reserved?	*Kore wa shtay-seki des-ka?* これは指定席ですか?
Could you tell me where to get off for Osaka?	*Osaka e iku ni-wa, doko de oriru-ka oshie-tay kuda-sai.* 大阪市へ行くには、どこで降りるか教えてください。
Could you let me know when we get to Osaka?	*Osaka ni tswee-tara oshie-tay kuda-sai.* 大阪市に着いたら教えてください。

Where is the Shinkansen (bullet train) ticket office?	*Shinkansen no kippu-uriba wa doko des-ka?* 新幹線の切符売り場はどこですか？
I would like to buy a ticket to Tokyo.	*Tokyo maday no kippu o kai-tai des.* 東京までの切符を買いたい。。
I have a Japan Rail Pass.	*JR pas o mot-tay imas.* JRパス を持っています。
I would like to activate my Japan Rail Pass.	*JR pas o katsuyoo shi-tai des.* JRパス を活用したいです。
Here is my Exchange Order.	*Koray ga hikikae-shoh des.* これが引換証です。
Can I come back on the same ticket?	*Kono kippu wa ohfuku des-ka?* この切符は往復ですか？
Can I change (trains) on this ticket?	*Kono kippu de norikae-raremas-ka?* この切符で乗り換えられますか？
How long is this ticket valid for?	*Kono kippu wa its maday yookoh des-ka?* この切符はいつまで有効ですか？
How long will the journey take?	*Idoh ni dono kurai kakari mas-ka?* 移動にどのくらいかかりますか？
Can I use my Japan Rail Pass to go from Osaka to Kobe?	*Osaka kara Kobe maday JR pas ga tsukae-mas-ka?* 大阪から神戸までJRパスが使えますか？
Where can I get a SUICA/PASMO card?	*Suika/Pasumo wa doko de kaemas-ka?* スイカ／パスモはどこで買えますか？
Could you stop at the next stop, please?	*Tsugi no bas-tay de oroshtay kuda-sai.* 次のバス停で降ろしてください。
Where are we now?	*Ima dono-hen des-ka?* 今どのへんですか？
Do I have to get off here?	*Koko de ori-nakere-ba nari-masen ka?* ここで降りなければなりませんか？
Have we already passed...?	*Moh ... o tohri-mashta-ka?* もう…を通りましたか？
How long have I been asleep?	*Watashi wa dono gurai nemuri-mashta-ka?* 私はどのぐらい眠りましたか？
How long does...stop here?	*... wa koko ni dono-kurai tomat-tay imas-ka?* …はここにどのくらい止まっていますか？

6.2 Immigration and Customs

A passport is necessary for all visitors to Japan. Citizens of most European, North American and many Asian countries, as well as Australia and New Zealand, do not need a visa if they are staying as tourists or on business trips for up to 90 days. Drugs, firearms, and pornography may not be taken into Japan. Non-residents can bring in up to 400 cigarettes, 100 cigars, or 500g of tobacco; 2oz of perfume; and other goods up to 200,000 yen (about US$2,000) in value duty-free. Personal possessions are exempt.

I'm going to Hokkaido for vacation.	*Kyooka de Hokkaido e ikimas.* 休暇で北海道へ行きます。
I'm on a business trip.	*Shut-choh des.* 出張です。
I don't know how long I'll be staying yet.	*Dono-gurai tai-zai suru-ka mada wakari-masen.* どのぐらい滞在するかまだ分かりません。
I'll be staying for a weekend.	*Kono shoo-mats dakay imas.* この週末だけいます。
I'll be staying for a few days.	*Ni-san-nichi dakay imas.* 二、三日だけいます。
I'll be staying for a week.	*Is-shookan dakay imas.* 一週間だけいます。
I'll be staying for two weeks.	*Ni-shookan dakay imas.* 二週間だけいます。
I have nothing to declare.	*Nani-mo shinkoku suru mono wa arimasen.* 何も申告する物はありません。
I have...with me.	*... o mot-tay imas.* …を持っています。
I have 100 cigarettes.	*Tabako wa hyap-pon arimas.* たばこは百本あります。
I have a bottle of red wine.	*Aka-wain wa ip-pon arimas.* 赤ワインは一本あります。
I have some souvenirs.	*Omiyagay ga sukoshi arimas.* おみやげが少しあります。

These are (my) personal possessions.
Koray wa jibun de tsukau mono des.
これは自分で使う物です。

These are not new.
Koray wa atara-shiku arimasen.
これは新しくありません。

Here's the receipt.
Ryohshoo-sho des. 領収書です。

How much import tax do I have to pay?
Yunyoo-zay wa ikura des-ka?
輸入税はいくらですか?

Can I go now?
It-tay mo ee des-ka?
行ってもいいですか?

6.3 Luggage

Porter!
Pohtah-san! ポーターさん!

Could you take this luggage to...?
Kono nimots o ... ni mot-tay it-tay kuda-sai.
この荷物を…に持って行ってください。

How much do I owe you? *Ikura des-ka?* いくらですか?

Where can I find a luggage cart?
Daisha wa doko ni arimas-ka?
台車はどこにありますか?

Could you store this luggage for me?
Kono nimots o azukat-tay morae-mas-ka?
この荷物を預かってもらえますか?

Where are the luggage lockers?
Rokkah wa doko des-ka?
ロッカーはどこですか?

I can't get the locker open. *Rokkah ga aki-masen.*
ロッカーが空きません。

How much is it per item per day?
Ichi-nichi ik-ko ikura des-ka?
一日一個いくらですか?

How long can I leave my luggage here?
Watashi wa dono kurai koko ni nimots o oite-oku koto ga dekimas-ka?
私はどれくらいここに荷物を置いておくことができますか?

This is not my bag.
Watashi no kaban de-wa arimasen.
私のカバンではありま せん。

There's one bag missing still.
Kaban ga hitots tarimasen.
カバンが一つ足りません。

My suitcase is damaged.	*Soots-kehs ga kowarete-imasu.* スーツケースが壊れています。
My luggage has not arrived.	*Watashi no nimots ga todoite-masen.* 私の荷物が届いていません。
When do you think my luggage will arrive?	*Watashi no nimots wa its todoku-n desho-ka?* 私の荷物はいつ届くんでしょうか?
Can I get any compensation during this time as my belongings are all in the luggage?	*Shoji-hin wa subete nimots no naka nano-de sono aida, hoshoh shtay morae-mas-ka?* 所持品はすべて荷物の中なので、その間、保証してもらえますか?
Can you please send my luggage to this address?	*Kono joosho ni nimotsu-o okutte-kuda-sai.* この住所に荷物を送ってください。
The lock has been broken.	*Kagi ga kowarete-imas.* 鍵が壊れています。
Where is the luggage forwarding service?	*Nimots no tensoh sahbisu wa doko des-ka?* 荷物の転送サービスはどこですか?
How soon will I get my luggage?	*Dono kurai de nimots ga todoki mas-ka?* どのくらいで荷物が届きますか?
Does it cost more for same-day delivery?	*Sokujits haisoh no ryohkin wa motto kakarimas-ka?* 即日配送の料金はもっとかかりますか?

6.4 Questions to passengers

Ticket types

Eチケット	e-ticket	この切符は…ですか。	Is this ticket...?
一等	first class	二等	second class
片道	one-way	往復	round-trip
喫煙車	smoking	禁煙車	no-smoking
窓側の座席	window	通路側の座席	aisle
列車の前方	front	列車の後方	back
座席	seat	寝台車	berth

上 top
中 middle
下 bottom
エコノミークラスまたはビジネスクラス?
　Tourist class or business class?
個室または座席? Cabin or seat?
一人用または二人用? Single or double?
何人ですか? How many are traveling?

Destination

どこへ行きますか? Where are you traveling to?
いつ出発しますか? When are you leaving?
…に出発します。 Your... leaves at...
乗り換えなければなりません。 You have to change trains.
…で降りなければなりません。 You have to get off at...
…経由で行かなければなりません。 You have to travel via...
出発は…です。 The outward journey is on...
帰りは…です。 The return journey is on...
…までに乗船しなければなりません。
　You have to be on board by....

Inside the train, plane or bus

切符を見せてください。 Your ticket, please.
指定席券を見せてください。 Your reservation, please.
パスポートを見せてください。 Your passport, please.
座席が違います。 You're in the wrong seat.
… が違います。 You're on/in the wrong...
これは指定席です。 This seat is reserved.
別料金を払わなければなりません。
　You'll have to pay an extra fare.
…は…分遅れています。
　The...has been delayed by... (how many) minutes.

6.5 Tickets

Where can I buy a ticket?	*Kippu wa doko de kae-mas-ka?* 切符はどこで買えますか?
Where can I make a reservation?	*Doko de yoyaku dekimas-ka?* どこで予約出来ますか?
Where can I reserve a flight?	*Hikohki no kippu wa doko de kae-mas-ka?* 飛行機の切符はどこで買えますか?
Could I have a one-way ticket, please?	*Katamichi no kippu onegai shimas.* 片道の切符お願いします。
Could I have a round-trip ticket, please?	*Ohfuku no kippu onegai shimas.* 往復の切符お願いします。
Could I have a first class ticket, please?	*It-toh-sha no kippu onegai shimas.* 一等車の切符お願いします。
Could I have a second class ticket, please?	*Ni-toh-sha no kippu onegai shimas.* 二等車の切符お願いします。
Could I have an economy class ticket, please?	*Ekonomee-kuras no kippu onegai shimas.* エコノミークラスの切符お願いします。
Could I have a business class ticket, please?	*Bijines-kuras no kippu onegai shimas.* ビジネスクラスの切符お願いします。
I'd like to reserve a seat.	*Zaseki o yoyaku shi-tai-n des.* 座席を予約したいんです。
I'd like to reserve a berth.	*Shin-dai-sha o yoyaku shi-tai-n des.* 寝台車を予約したいんです。
I'd like to reserve aisle seats.	*Tsu-ro gawa no seki o yoyaku shi-tai-n des.* 通路側の席を予約したいんです。
I'd like to reserve the top bunk.	*Weh no shin-dai o yoyaku shi-tai-n des ga.* 上の寝台を予約したいんですが。
I'd like to reserve the middle bunk.	*Naka no shin-dai o yoyaku shi-tai-n des ga.* 中の寝台を予約したいんですが。
I'd like to reserve the bottom bunk.	*Shta no shin-dai o yoyaku shi-tai-n des ga.* 下の寝台を予約したいんですが。
I'd like to reserve a cabin.	*Sen-shits o yoyaku shi-tai-n des ga.* 船室を予約したいんですが。

I'd like to reserve a
smoking seat.

Kitsu-en no seki o yoyaku shi-tai-n des ga.
喫煙の席を予約したいんですが。

I'd like to reserve a
no-smoking seat.

Kin'en no seki o yoyaku shi-tai-n des ga.
禁煙の席を予約したいんですが。

I'd like to reserve a seat
by the window.

Mado-giwa-no seki o yoyaku shi-tai-n des ga.
窓際の席を予約したいんですが。

I'd like to reserve a seat
at the front of the train.

*Ressha no zempoh no seki o yoyaku
shi-tai-n des ga.*
列車の前方の席を予約したいんですが。

I'd like to reserve a seat
at the back of the train.

*Ressha no koh-hoh no seki o yoyaku
shi-tai-n des ga.*
列車の後方の席予約したいんですが。

I'd like to reserve a seat
at the front of the plane.

*Hikohki no zempoh no seki o yoyaku
shi-tai-n des ga.*
飛行機の前方の席予約したいんですが。

I'd like to reserve a seat
at the back of the plane.

*Hikohki no koh-hoh no seki o yoyaku
shi-tai-n des ga.*
飛行機の後方の席予約したいんですが。

Do you also have
season tickets?

Tayki-ken mo arimas-ka?
定期券もありますか？

6.6 Information

Where's the
information desk?

An-nai-jo wa doko des-ka?
案内所はどこですか？

Where can I find
a schedule?

Jikoku-hyoh wa doko des-ka?
時刻表はどこですか？

Do you have a city
map with the bus/the
subway routes on it?

*Bas-ya/chika-tets ga not-tay iru
machi no chizu wa arimas-ka?*
バスや／地くだ鉄が載っている町の地
図はありますか？

Do you have a schedule?

Jikoku-hyoh arimas-ka?
時刻表ありますか？

I'd like to confirm my
trip to Osaka.

*Osaka maday no ryokoh o tashi-kametay-n
des.*
大阪までの旅行を確かめたいんです。

I'd like to confirm my reservation for Osaka.	*Osaka maday no yoyaku o tashi-kametay-n des.* 大阪までの予約を確かめたいんです。
I'd like to cancel my trip to Kyoto.	*Kyoto maday no ryokoh o torikeshi-tai-n des.* 京都までの旅行を取り消したいんです。
I'd like to cancel my reservation for Kyoto.	*Kyoto maday no yoyaku o torikeshi-tai-n des.* 京都までの予約を取り消したいんです。
I'd like to change my trip to Tokyo.	*Tokyo maday no ryokoh o kae-tai-n des.* 東京までの旅行を変えたいんです。
I'd like to change my reservation for Tokyo.	*Tokyo maday no yoyaku o kae-tai-n des.* 東京までの予約を変えたいんです。
Will I get my money back?	*Ha-rai modoshi o saykyoo dekimas-ka?* 払戻しを請求出来ますか?
I want to go to Osaka. How do I get there?	*Osaka e iki-tai-n des-ga, dono-yoh ni ikimas-ka?* 大阪へ行きたいんですが、どのように行きますか?
What is the quickest way there?	*Nani ga ichiban ha-yai des-ka?* 何が一番早いですか?
Do I have to pay extra?	*Tswee-ka ryohkin o harawa-nakereba nari-masen-ka?* 追加料金を払わなければなりませんか?
How much is a single (trip ticket) to Tokyo?	*Tokyo maday no katamichi wa ikura des-ka?* 東京までの片道はいくらですか?
How much is a return (trip ticket) to Tokyo?	*Tokyo maday no ohfu-ku wa ikura des-ka?* 東京までの往復はいくらですか?
Can I interrupt my journey with this ticket?	*Kono kippu de tochoo-gesha ga dekimas-ka?* この切符で途中くだ車が出来ますか?
How much luggage am I allowed?	*Nimots wa nan-kiro maday mot-tay ikemas-ka?* 荷物は何キロまで持って行けますか?
Can I send my luggage in advance?	*Nimots o takuhai-bin de okuremas-ka?* 荷物を宅配便で送れますか?

Does this bus travel direct?	*Kono bas wa chok-koh des-ka?* このバスは直行ですか?
Do I have to change? Where (do I change)?	*Norikae-nakereba-nari-masen-ka?* *Doko-de?* 乗り換えなければなりませんか?どこで?
Will there be any stopovers?	*Dokoka tochoo tachiyorimas-ka?* どこか途中立ち寄りますか?
Does the boat call at any ports on the way?	*Tochoo minato ni kikoh shimas-ka?* 途中港に寄港しますか?
Does the train/bus stop at Kobe?	*Kono densha/bas wa Kobe ni tomarimas-ka?* この電車／バスは神戸に止まりますか?
Where should I get off?	*Doko de ori-nakereba nari-masen-ka?* どこで降りなければなりませんか?
Is there a connection to...?	*... maday no setsu-zoku wa arimas-ka?* …までの接続はありますか?
How long do I have to wait?	*Dono gurai mata-nakereba nari-masen-ka?* どのぐらい待たなければなりませんか?
When does the train leave?	*Densha wa its shuppats shimas-ka?* 電車はいつ出発しますか?
What time does the next train leave?	*Tsugi no densha wa nan-ji ni shuppats shimas-ka?* 次の電車は何時に出発しますか?
What time does the last train leave?	*Sai-shoo no densha wa nan-ji ni shuppats shimas-ka?* 最終の電車は何時に出発しますか?
How long does (the trip) take?	*Dono-gurai kakarimas-ka?* どのぐらいかかりますか?
What time does the train arrive in Kobe?	*Kobe ni nan-ji densha ni tsukimas-ka?* 神戸に何時電車に着きますか?
Where does the train to Kobe leave from?	*Kobe ni iki no densha wa doko-kara shuppats shimas-ka?* 神戸に行きの電車はどこから出発しますか?

Is this the train/bus to...? *Koray wa ... iki no densha/bas des-ka?*
これは…行きの電車／バスですか?

6.7 Airports

arrivals	Internet lounge	airport hotels
tohchaku	*Intah-netto raunji*	*kookoh-nai hoteru*
到着	インターネットラウンジ	空港内ホテル
departures	airport security	metal detector
shuppats	*koo-koh keibi/koo-koh*	*kinzoku tanchi-ki*
出発	*sekyuritee*	金属探知機
international	空港警備／空港セキュリ	baggage claim
kokusai	ティー	*tenimots*
国際	e-booking/reservations	*uketori-sho*
domestic	*ee-bukkingu*	手荷物受取所
kokunai	E-ブッキング	pacemaker
国内	checking in	*peh-su-maykah*
scanner	*chekku-in*	ペースメーカー
sukyanah	チェックイン	security
スキャナー	baggage claim check	*sekyuritee*
boarding pass	*tenimots hikikae-ken*	セキュリティー
tohjohken	手荷物引換券	
搭乗券		

6.8 Trains

The railway system in Japan is very well developed, and managed by Japan Railways (JR) and a large number of private railway companies. Intercity trains are local (*futsoo*), express (*kyoo-koh*), limited express (*tok-kyoo*), and super express (*shinkansen*).

Tickets are charged by distance, with surcharges for the category of train, class, and seat reservations. Ticket reservations are made at counters called 'green windows' (*midori no madoguchi*). Tickets can be bought from ticket machines and most of these have an English option. The full fare does not have to be paid before the destination. Fare adjustment machines and counters are available so you can pay the difference when you arrive. All JR stations show station names written in Japanese with the romanization below. Useful for travelers is the custom of including the names of the previous and next stations to the left and right underneath the station name.

Taxis

Taxis are expensive, but are always metered and there is no custom of tipping. Carry the address and phone number of your destination written in Japanese, and a map of the immediate location if possible, to give to the driver. Taxi doors are automated; normally the back curbside door is the only one used. On arrival, wait for the driver to open the door on the left-hand side of the taxi, and do not close it yourself when you get in or out of the taxi. Let the driver do it.

for hire	booked	taxi stand
koosha	*johshachoo*	*tak-shee noriba*
空車	乗車中	タクシー乗り場

Taxi!	*Tak-shee!* タクシー！
Could you get me a taxi, please?	*Tak-shee o yonday kuda-sai.* タクシーを呼んでください。
Where can I find a taxi around here?	*Tak-shee noriba wa doko des-ka?* タクシー乗り場はどこですか？
Could you take me to this address, please?	*Kono joosho maday o-negai shimas.* この住所までお願いします。
Could you take me to the...hotel, please?	*... hoteru maday o-negai shimas.* …ホテルまでお願いします。
Could you take me to town/ the city center, please?	*Choo-shin-chi maday o-negai shimas.* 中心地までお願いします。
Could you take me to the train station, please?	*Eki maday o-negai shimas.* 駅までお願いします。
Could you take me to the airport, please?	*Kookoh maday o-negai shimas.* 空港までお願いします。
How much is the trip to Narita Airport?	*Narita kookoh maday ikura des-ka?* 成田空港までいくらですか？

How far is it to Narita airport?	*Narita kookoh maday nan-kiro gurai des-ka?* 成田空港まで何キロぐらいですか?
I'm in a hurry.	*Isoi-de iru-n des-ga.* 急いでいるんですが。
Could you speed up a little?	*Motto hayakuit-tay kuda-sai.* もっと速く行ってください。
Could you slow down a little?	*Motto yuk-kuri it-tay kuda-sai.* もっとゆっくり行ってください。
Could you take a different route?	*Hoka no michi de it-tay kuda-sai.* 他の道で行ってください。
I'd like to get out here, please.	*Koko de oroshtay kuda-sai.* ここで降ろしてください。
You have to go straight.	*Massugu it-tay kuda-sai.* 真っ直ぐ行ってください。
You have to turn left.	*Hidari ni magat-tay kuda-sai.* 左に曲がってください。
You have to turn right.	*Migi ni magat-tay kuda-sai.* 右に曲がってください。
It's on the opposite side of the road.	*Michi no hantai-gawa des.* 道の反対側です。
This is it.	*Koko des.* ここです。
Could you wait a minute for me, please?	*Chotto mat-tay-tay kuda-sai.* ちょっと待っててください。
I need to make a stop here.	*Koko de tomete kuda-sai.* ここで止めてください。
I'll be right back.	*Sugu ni modori-mas.* すぐに戻ります。
Could you help me open the boot so I can get my luggage?	*Kuruma no toranku o akete morae-masen-ka? Nimots o tori-tai-n des.* 車のトランクを開けてもらえませんか? 荷物を取りたいんです。
Could you help me carry my luggage to the taxi?	*Tak-shee maday nimots o hakonde morae-masen-ka?* タクシーまで荷物を運んでもらえ ませんか?

7. A Place to Stay

General

Japan has a wide range of hotels, from five-star international hotels to small business hotels and local inns. The cheaper the hotel, the smaller the room and the fewer the facilities. Whatever the grade of hotel, cleanliness is likely to be high. Other accommodation, especially in country areas, includes the very expensive luxury *ryokan* (traditional inns) and small, cheaper inns.

Inns are a good way to experience the Japanese lifestyle. Rooms are covered with straw mats (*tatami*) and the guest sleeps on a futon spread on the floor. In luxury inns, Japanese-style meals are served in the room. Bathing is generally communal—male and female facilities are separated—in a large room containing a sunken, very hot bath for relaxation and individual taps and stools to wash yourself prior to entering the bath. In rural areas these baths may be *onsen* (volcanic hot springs).

Many small inns now operate as *minshuku*, inexpensive accommodation offering two meals. These can be booked through the travel counters at stations and airports, or through the Internet. They are a good option especially when traveling in the countryside. In the last few years a western version called *pension* has also become popular. Camping is not popular, and campsites are few and poor in the way of facilities. Other affordable alternatives include youth hostels, capsule hotels and apartments (or single rooms, if you prefer) for rent from sites like Airbnb.

いつまでお泊まりですか? How long will you be staying?
この用紙に記入してください。 Fill in this form, please.
パスポートをお願いします。 Could I see your passport?
保証金をお願いします。 I'll need a deposit.
前払いでお願いします。 You'll have to pay in advance.

My name's...I've made a reservation.	*Watashi wa ... des. Heya no yoyaku o shtay arimas.* 私は…です。部屋の予約をしてあります。
I've made a reservation over the phone.	*Denwa-de yoyaku shimashta.* 電話で予約しました。
I've booked a room from a booking website.	*Webu-saito de yoyaku-shimashta.* ウェブサイトで予約しました。
I've booked a room from your hotel website.	*Hoteru no saito de yoyaku-shimashta.* ホテルのサイトで予約しました。
I've made a reservation by email.	*May-ru de yoyaku shimashta.* メールで予約しました。
Here's my booking confirmation.	*Koko ni yoyaku kakunin-sho ga-arimas.* ここに私の予約確認があります。
How much per night?	*Ip-paku wa ikura des-ka?* 一泊はいくらですか?
How much per week?	*Is-shookan wa ikura des-ka?* 一週間はいくらですか?
How much per month?	*Ik-ka-gets wa ikura des-ka?* 一ヶ月はいくらですか?
We'll be staying for at least two nights.	*Semetay ni-haku tomari-tai-n des-ga.* せめて二泊泊まりたいんですが。
We'll be staying for at least two weeks.	*Semetay ni-shookan tomari-tai-n des-ga.* せめて二週間泊まりたいんですが。
We don't know yet.	*Mada wakari-masen-ga.* まだ分かりませんが。
What time does the gate/door open?	*Nan-ji ni akimas-ka?* 何時に開きますか?

What time does the gate/door close?	*Nan-ji ni shimarimas-ka?* 何時に閉まりますか？

7.2 Hotels/B&Bs/apartments/holiday rentals

Do you have a single room?	*Hitori-beya arimas-ka?* 一人部屋ありますか？
Do you have a double room?	*Ftari-beya arimas-ka?* 二人部屋ありますか？
How much per person?	*Hitori-ni-tski ikura des ka?* 一人に付きいくらですか？
How much per room?	*Hito-heya-ni-tski ikura des ka?* 一部屋に付きいくらですか？
Does that include breakfast?	*Choh-shoku-tski des-ka?* 朝食付きですか？
Does that include lunch?	*Choo-shoku-tski des-ka?* 昼食付きですか？
Does that include dinner?	*Yoo-shoku-tski des-ka?* 夕食付きですか？
Could we have two adjoining rooms?	*Tonari-awase no heya arimas-ka?* 隣り合わせの部屋ありますか？
Could we have a room with toilet/bath/shower?	*Toire/bas/shawah-tski no heya arimas-ka?* トイレ／バス／シャワー付きの部屋 ありますか？
Could we have a room facing the street?	*Michi ni men-shtay iru heya arimas-ka?* 道に面している部屋ありますか？
Could we have a room not facing the street?	*Michi ni men-shtay-nai heya arimas-ka?* 道に面してない部屋ありますか？
Could we have a room with a view of the sea?	*Umi-gawa no heya arimas-ka?* 海側の部屋ありますか？
Could we have a room without a sea view?	*Umi ni men-shtay-nai heya arimas-ka?* 海に面してない部屋ありますか？
Is there an elevator in the hotel?	*Erebehtah wa arimas-ka?* エレベーターはありますか？
Do you have room service?	*Room-sahbis wa arimas-ka?* ルームサービスはありますか？

Do you have accommodation without meals?	*Sudomari wa arimas-ka?* 素泊まりはありますか?
Could I see the room?	*Heya o misetay moraemas-ka?* 部屋を見せてもらえますか?
I'll take this room.	*Kono-heya ni kime-mashta.* この部屋に決めました。
Please show us another room.	*Hoka no heya o misetay kuda-sai.* 他の部屋を見せてください。
Do you have a larger room?	*Motto ohkee heya wa arimasen-ka?* もっと大きい部屋はありませんか?
Do you have a less expensive room?	*Motto yaswee heya wa arimasen-ka?* もっと安い部屋はありませんか?
Could you add an extra bed?	*Kodomo-yoh no beddo o tsweeka dekimas-ka?* 子供用のベッドを追加できますか?
What time's breakfast?	*Choh-shoku wa nan-ji des-ka?* 朝食は何時ですか?

トイレやバスは同階／部屋にあります。 You can find the toilet
　and shower on the same floor/in the room.
こちらです。 This way, please.
…階にあります。 Your room is on the...floor.
お部屋は…号室です。 Your room is number....

Where's the dining room?	*Shokudoh wa doko des-ka?* 食堂はどこですか?
Can I have breakfast in my room?	*Choh-shoku o heya de taberare-mas-ka?* 朝食を部屋で食べられますか?
Where's the emergency exit?	*Hijoh-guchi wa doko des-ka?* 非常口はどこですか?
Where's the fire escape?	*Hijoh-kai-dan wa doko des-ka?* 非常階段はどこですか?
Where can I park my car?	*Doko ni choo-sha dekimas-ka?* どこに駐車出来ますか?

The key to room..., please	*...goh shits no kagi onegai shimas.* …号室の鍵お願いします。
Could you put this in the safe, please?	*Koray o kinko ni iretay kuda-sai-mas-ka?* これを金庫に入れてくださいますか?
Could you wake me at 8am tomorrow?	*Ashta hachi ji ni okoshtay kuda-sai.* 明日8時に起こしてください。
Could you find a babysitter for me?	*Bebee-shittah o onegai dekimas-ka?* ベビーシッターをお願い出来ますか?
Could I have an extra blanket?	*Mohfu o moh ichi-mai onegai shimas.* 毛布をもう一枚お願いします。
What days do the cleaners come in?	*Osohji wa nan-yohbi des-ka?* お掃除は何曜日ですか?
When are the sheets changed?	*Its sheets o tori-kae-mas-ka?* いつシーツを取り替えますか?
When are the towels changed?	*Its taoru o tori-kae-mas-ka?* いつタオルを取り替えますか?

7.3 Complaints

We can't sleep because it's too noisy.	*Uru-saku-tay nemure-nai-n des.* うるさくて眠れないんです。
Could you turn the radio down, please?	*Rajio no onryoh o sagetay kuda-sai.* ラジオの音量をくだげてください。
We're out of toilet paper.	*Toyretto-pehpah ga nai-n des-ga.* トイレットペーパーがないんですが。
There aren't any...	*... ga tari-nai-n des.* …が足りないんです。
The bed linen's dirty.	*Sheets ga kita-nai-n des-ga.* シーツがきたないんですが。
The room hasn't been cleaned.	*Heya ga sohji shtay-masen.* 部屋が掃除してません。
The heater's not working.	*Damboh ga kee-te imasen.* 暖房が効いていません。
The air conditioning's not working.	*E-a-kon ga kee-te imasen.* エアコンが効いていません。
There's no water.	*Mizu ga de-masen.* 水が出ません。

There's no hot water.	*Oyu ga de-masen.* お湯が出ません。
There's no electricity.	*Denki ga tsuki-masen.* 電気がつきません。
...is broken	*... ga kowaretay imas.* …がこわれています。
Could you have that fixed?	*Sono-yoh ni onegai shimas.* そのようにお願いします。
Could I have another room/site?	*Hoka no heya ni ka-etay kuda-sai.* 他の部屋に替えてください。
The bed creaks terribly.	*Beddo ga kishim-n des-ga.* ベッドがきしむんですが。
The bed sags.	*Beddo ga yawaraka-sugimas.* ベッドが柔らか過ぎます。
There are bugs/insects in our room.	*Heya ni mushi ga iru-n des-ga.* 部屋に虫がいるんですが。
This place is full of mosquitos.	*Koko ni wa ka ga takusan itay, komarimas.* ここには蚊がたくさんいて、こまります。
This place is full of cockroaches.	*Koko ni wa go-kiburi ga takusan itay,* *komarimas.* ここにはゴキブリがたくさんいて、 こまります。

7.4 Departure

See also 8.2 Settling the bill

I'm leaving tomorrow. Could I pay the bill, please?	*Ashta tachi-mas-kara saysan shtay* *kuda-sai.* 明日立ちますから、精算してください。
What time should we check out?	*Nan-ji maday ni chekku-auto shinakereba* *nari-masen-ka?* 何時までにチェックアウトしなければ なりませんか?
Could I have my deposit back, please?	*Hoshoh-kin o kae-shtay kuda-sai.* 保証金を返してください。
Could I have my passport back, please?	*Paspohto o kae-shtay kuda-sai.* パスポートを返してください。

We're in a rush.	*Tai-hen isoi-de imas.* 大変急いでいます。
Could we leave our luggage here until we leave?	*Shuppats-maday nimots o koko ni oitay mo ee des-ka?* 出発まで荷物をここに置いてもいいですか？
Thanks for your hospitality.	*Omotenashi, arigatoh gozai-mashta.* おもてなし、ありがとうございました。

7.5 Camping

See the diagram on page 92

ご自分で場所を決めてください。 You can pick your own site.
場所が割り当てられています。 You'll be allocated a site.
あなたの場所の番号です。 This is your site number.
自動車に貼り付けてください。 Stick this on your car, please.

Where's the manager?	*Kanri-nin wa doko des-ka?* 管理人はどこですか？
Are we allowed to camp here?	*Koko de kyamp dekimas-ka?* ここでキャンプ出来ますか？
Can we pick our own site?	*Jibun de basho o kimetay mo ee des-ka?* 自分で場所を決めてもいいですか？
Do you have a quiet spot for us?	*Shizuka na basho ga arimas-ka?* 静かな場所がありますか？
Do you have any other sites available?	*Hoka ni basho ga arimasen-ka?* 他に場所がありませんか？
The ground's too hard/uneven.	*Jimen ga kata-sugimas/deko-boko des.* 地面が堅過ぎます／でこぼこです。
Do you have a level spot for the camper/trailer/folding trailer?	*Kyamping-kah no tamay ni taira na basho ga arimas-ka?* キャンピングカーのために平らな場所がありますか？
It's too crowded here.	*Koko wa komi-sugi-tay imas.* ここは混み過ぎています。

It's too windy/sunny here.   *Koko wa kazay/hizashi ga tsuyo-sugi-mas.*
ここは風／日ざしが強過ぎます。

Could we have
adjoining sites?   *Issho ni tate-rareru basho ga arimas-ka?*
一緒に立てられる場所がありますか?

Can we park the car
next to the tent?   *Tento no tonari ni choosha shtay mo
ee des-ka?*
テントの隣に駐車してもいいですか?

How much is it per
trailer?   *Kyamping-kah ichi-dai wa ikura des-ka?*
キャンピングカー一台はいくらですか?

Are there any hot
showers?   *Oyu no shawah arimas-ka?*
お湯のシャワーありますか?

Are there any washing
machines?   *Sentak-ki arimas-ka?*
洗濯機ありますか?

Is there a children's
play area on the site?   *Kyamp-joh ni wa kodomo-yoh no
asobiba ga arimas-ka?*
キャンプ場には、子供用の遊び場が
ありますか?

Can I rent a locker here?   *Rokkah ga kari-raremas-ka?*
ロッカーが借りられますか?

Are there any
power outlcts?   *Denki o tsuka-e-mas-ka?*
電気を使えますか?

Is there drinking water?   *Nomi-mizu wa arimas-ka?*
飲み水はありますか?

When's the garbage
(usually) collected?   *Gomi wa its atsume-mas-ka?*
ごみはいつ集めますか?

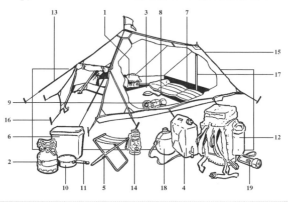

Camping equipment

(The diagram on page 92 shows the numbered items.)

	can opener	かん切り	*kan-kiri*
	butane gas bottle	ブタン・ガスボンベ	*butan-gas-bombay*
	hammer	かなづち	*kana-zuchi*
	hammock	ハンモック	*hammok*
	campfire	キャンプファイヤー	*kyamp fai-yah*
	ice pack	アイスパック	*ais-pakku*
	compass	コンパス	*kompas*
	wick	芯	*shin*
	corkscrew	コルク抜き	*kork-nuki*
	pump	空気入れ	*kooki-iray*
	primus stove	コンロ	*konro*
	zip	ファスナー／ジッパー	*fasnah/jippah*
	camp bed	キャンプ用ベッド	*kyamp-yoh beddo*
	table	折りたたみ式（キャンプ用）テーブル	*oritatami-shki (kyamp-yoh) tehburu*
	thermos	魔法瓶	*ma-hoh-bin*
	clothes hook	洗濯バサミ	*sentaku-basami*
	clothes line	物干しロープ	*monohoshi rohp*
	pocket knife	小刀	*kogatana*
1	tool bag	自転車用バッグ	*jitensha-yoh bag-gu*
2	gas cooker	ガス・コンロ	*gas-konro*
3	groundsheet	グランドシート	*gurando sheeto*
4	gas can	燃料タンク	*nenryoh-tank*
5	folding chair	折りたたみイス	*oritatami-isu*
6	insulated picnic box	クーラー・ボックス	*koorah bokks*
7	airbed	エア・マットレス	*e-a mattres*
8	airbed plug	プラグ	*prag*
9	mat	マットレス	*mattres*
10	pan	鍋	*nabay*
11	pan handle	鍋つかみ	*nabay tskami*
12	backpack	リュックサック	*ryukk-sakk*
13	guy rope/rope	ロープ	*rohpu*
14	storm lantern	ランタン／灯油ランプ	*rantan/toh-yoo ramp*
15	tent	テント	*tento*
16	tent peg	ペグ	*pegg*
17	tent pole	テント・ポール	*tento-pohru*
18	water bottle	水筒	*sweetoh*
19	flashlight	懐中電灯／ポケットライト	*kai-choo den-toh/ pokett-raito*

8. Money Matters

8.1 Banks and getting money
8.2 Settling the bill

In general, banks are open Monday–Friday 9am–3pm. They are closed on Saturdays, Sundays, and national holidays. Many shops and restaurants in Japan only accept cash, so it is a good idea to always carry sufficient Japanese yen with you. In many smaller towns, the Post Office serves as the local bank. Hotels will change money but the rate is not good and they only accept certain currencies, so it is best to go to a bank when changing large amounts. Cash can be obtained by withdrawing money from your credit card at ATM machines in selected convenience stores like 7-11 and Lawsons in city areas.

Banks and getting money

Where can I find a bank?	*Ginkohwa doko des-ka?* 両替所はどこですか?
Where can I find an exchange office?	*Ryohgae-jo wa doko des-ka?* 辺に銀行はどこですか?
Where can I find an ATM machine?	*Kono-hen ni ATM (ay-tee-emu) wa doko des-ka?* この辺にATMはどこですか?
What are the charges for withdrawing money from this ATM?	*ATM (ay-tee-emu) kara okanay o hiki-dasu te-soo-ryoh wa ikura des-ka?* ATMからお金を引き出す手数料はいくらですか?
Can I cash this...here?	*Kono ... wa koko de genkin ni kae-rare-mas-ka?* この…はここで現金に替えられますか?
I'd like to withdraw yen.	*Okanay o oroshi-tai-n des-ga.* お金をおろしたいのですが。

Can I withdraw cash from my credit card here?	*Krejitto-kahdo de genkin o hiki-dasemas-ka?* クレジットカードで現金を引き出せますか？
What's the minimum/maximum amount?	*Sai-shoh/sai-koh-gaku wa ikura des-ka?* 最小／最高額はいくらですか？
Can I get less/more than that?	*Skoshi-demo ee des-ka?* 少しでもいいですか？
This is my bank account number.	*Koray wa watashi no kohza bangoh des.* これは私の口座番号です。
What's the exchange rate?	*Kawasay rayto wa ikura des-ka?* 為替レートはいくらですか？
I'd like to change some money.	*Okanay o ryoh-gae shi-tai-n des-ga.* お金を両替したいんですが。
– pounds into yen	*pondo o yen-ni* ポンドを円に
– dollars into yen	*doru o yen-ni* ドルを円に
– euros into yen	*yooro o yen-ni* ユーロを円に
Could you give me some small bills/coins?	*Osatsu/kozeni mo iretay kuda-sai.* お札／小銭も入れてください。
This is not right.	*Machigat-tay iru-to omoimas-ga.* 間違っていると思いますが。

ここに署名してください。Sign here, please.
これに記入してください。Fill this out, please.
パスポートを見せてください。Could I see your passport, please?
身分証明書を見せてください。Could I see some identification, please?
バンクカード／キャッシュカードを見せてください。
Could I see your bank/cash card, please?

8.2 Settling the bill

How much is this?	*Ikura des-ka?* いくらですか？

Could you put it on my bill?	*Heya ni tsketay oitay kuda-sai.* 部屋に付けておいてください。
Does this amount include the tip?	*Sahbis-ryoh wa hait-tay imas-ka?* サービス料は入っていますか？
Can I pay by credit card?	*Krejitto-kahdo de harae-mas-ka?* クレジットカードで払えますか？
You've given me too much.	*Otsuri ga oh-sugimas.* おつりが多すぎます。
You haven't given me enough change.	*Otsuri ga tari-nai-n des-ga.* おつりが足りないんですが。
Could you check this again, please?	*Moh ichido tashi-kametay kuda-sai-masen-ka?* もう一度確かめてくださいませんか？
Could I have a receipt, please?	*Ryoh-shoo-sho onegai shimas.* 領収書お願いします。
I don't have enough money on me.	*Sumimasen, okanay ga tari-masen.* すみません、お金が足りません。
Do you accept Mastercard credit cards?	*Masutah kahdo wa tsukaemas-ka?* マスターカードは使えますか？
Do you accept VISA credit cards?	*Bi-sa wa tsukaemas-ka?* VISAは使えますか？
Do you accept American Express credit cards?	*Amerikan Ekus-pures wa tsukaemas-ka?* アメリカンエクスプレスは使えますか？

クレジットカードはご使用になれ ません。
　We don't accept credit cards.
外貨はご使用になれません。　We don't accept foreign currency.

This is for you.	*Dohzo.* どうぞ。
Keep the change.	*Otsuri wa tot-tay oitay kuda-sai.* お釣りはとっておいてください。
Please enter your PIN number.	*Ansho-bangoh o new-ryoku shtay kuda-sai.* 暗証番号を入力してください。

9. Mail, Phone and Internet

9.1 Mail
9.2 Telephone
9.3 Internet/email/social media

9.1 Mail

You can ask your hotel to help you send letters or parcels. Some shops catering to foreigners also can arrange to send parcels to your overseas address. Post offices open 9am–5pm Monday-Friday, with cash-related facilities available until 3pm. The main offices are also open on Saturday mornings, 9am–12.30pm. They are closed on Sundays and national holidays. However, they have after-hours services for designated items like foreign mail. Press the buzzer near the entrance and an attendant will come out to you. The Central Post Office across from Tokyo Station is open 24 hours a day. You can address letters using the English script (*romaji*).

money orders	parcels	stamps
yoobin-kawase	*yoobin-kodzutsumi*	*kit-tay*
郵便為替	郵便小包み	切手

Where's the post office?	*Kono-hen ni yoo-bin-kyoku wa arimas-ka?* この辺に郵便局はありますか？
Where's the mailbox?	*Kono-hen ni posto wa arimas-ka?* この辺にポストはありますか？
Where can I send a courier package?	*Doko de takuhai-bin o okuremas ka?* どこで宅配便を送れますか？
Can you help me send this package by courier?	*Kono nimots o takuhaibin de okuruk koto ga dekimas-ka?* この荷物を宅配便で送ることができますか？
What is the cost?	*Ikura des-ka?* いくらですか？

Stamps

What's the postage for a letter to America?	*Amerika maday no tegami wa ikura des-ka?* アメリカかまでの手紙はいくらですか？
What's the postage for a postcard to America?	*Amerika maday no hagaki wa ikura des-ka?* アメリカかまでの葉書はいくらですか？
Are there enough stamps on it?	*Kit-tay wa tarimas-ka?* 切手は足りますか？
I'd like two 50 yen stamps.	*Go-joo yen no kit-tay o ni-mai onegai shimas.* 50円の切手を二枚お願いします。
I'd like to send this by express mail.	*Kore o sokutats de onegai shimas.* これを速達でお願いします。
I'd like to send this by air mail.	*Kore o kohkoo-bin de onegai shimas.* これを航空便でお願いします。
I'd like to send this by registered mail.	*Kore o kaki-tomay de onegai shimas.* これを書留でお願いします。

Scanning/Photocopying

Shall I fill out the form myself?	*Yohshi ni jibun de ki-nyoo shimashoh-ka?* 用紙に自分で記入しましょうか？
Can I make photocopies here?	*Koko de kopee dekimas-ka?* ここでコピー出来ますか？
How much is it per page?	*Ip-peh-ji ikura des-ka?* 1ページいくらですか？
Can I scan this here?	*Kore o sukyan shi-tai no des-ga?* これをスキャンしたいのですが？

9.2 Telephone

If you have a smartphone, it should work on Japan's 3G and 4G networks, but data roaming will be costly. To get around this, you can install a Japanese data SIM card—your phone must be unlocked by your country's carrier before traveling to Japan—at the airport or from large electronic stores like Yodobashi. To make calls you can use apps like Skype or Viber.

If you intend to make a lot of domestic calls in Japan, it may be best to rent a mobile phone in Japan. It's best to do so at the airport on arrival since there will be English-speaking staff there who can guide you through the different rental packages and rates available. Most major airports have phone rental booths; ask at the information desk.

When making domestic calls, dial the whole number (including the 0 prefix). Toll-free calls can only be made from landlines. If you're calling overseas, first dial the international access code 010, followed by the country code (omit any 0s preceding the country code—dial 1 instead of 001 for the US and Canada, for example), and then the rest of the numbers.

Could I use your phone, please?	*Anata no denwa o karite-mo ee des-ka?* あなたの電話を借りてもいいですか?
Could you find a telephone number for me?	*Denwa-bangoh o shirabetay kuda-sai-masen-ka?* 電話番号を調べてくださいませんか?
Could you give me...?	*... o oshie-tay kuda-sai.* …を教えてください。
Could you give me Peter's room phone number?	*Peter-san no goh-shits no denwa-bangoh o oshie-tay kuda-sai.* 室の電話番号を教えてください。
What is the international access code?	*Kok-sai denwa no bangoh wa nan des ka?* 国際電話の番号は何ですか?
What is the country code for the UK?	*Igirisu no kuni bangoh wa nan des ka?* イギリスの国番号は何ですか?
What is the area code for Tokyo?	*Tokyo no shi-gai kyokuban wa nan des ka?* 東京の市外局番は何ですか?
Could you give me X restaurant's number?	*X no resutoran no denwa-bangoh o oshie-tay kuda-sai.* Xのレストランの電話番号を教えてください。
Could you check if this number is correct?	*Kono denwa-bangoh ga tada-shee-ka dohka shirabetay kuda-sai.* この電話番号が正しいかどうか調べてください。

Can I dial international (numbers) directly?
Gai-koku ni chokusets kakerare-mas-ka?
外国に直接掛けられますか？

Do I have to dial '0' first?
Sai-sho ni zero o oshi-mas-ka?
最初にゼロを押しますか？

Could you dial this number for me, please?
Kono denwa-bangoh ni tsunai de kuda-sai.
この電話番号につないでください。

Could you put me through to.../extension..., please?
...ban/naisen...ban ni tsunai de kuda-sai.
…番/内線…番につないでください。

I'd like to place a collect call to...
...ni korekt-kohru de denwa o kake-tai-n des-ga.
…にコレクトコールで電話をかけたいんですが。

What's the charge per minute?
Ip-pun-ni-tski ikura des-ka?
一分につきいくらですか？

Could I use my cell phone here?
Kokode kay-tai denwa o tsukat-tay mo ee des-ka?
ここで携帯電話を使ってもいいですか？

Do you have a smartphone?
Sumah-to fon o mot-tay imas-ka?
スマートフォンを持っていますか？

I have lost my (data) SIM card.
Shimu kahdo o naku-shtay shimai mashita.
SIMカードをなくしてしまいました。

I would like to buy a SIM card.
Shimu kahdo o kai-tai no des-ga.
SIMカードを買いたいのですが。

The signal is weak here.
Koko wa dempa ga yowai des.
ここは電波が弱いです。

Dead zone
Det-to zohn デッドゾーン

My battery is low.
Denchi/batteree ga sukunaku-nat-tay kite imas.
電池/バッテリーが少なくなくなってきています。

Where can I charge my cell phone?
Doko de kay-tai o joo-den dekimas-ka?
どこで携帯を充電できますか？

Can I text you later?
Ato de may-ru shtay mo ee des-ka?
後でメールしてもいいですか？

The conversation

Hello, this is...	*Mosh moshi, ... des.* もしもし、…です。
Who is this, please?	*Donata des-ka?* どなたですか?
Is this...?	*... san des-ka?* …さんですか?
I'm sorry, I've dialed the wrong number.	*Sumimasen-ga, machi-gat-tay kaketay shimai-mashta.* すみませんが、間違って掛けてしまいました。
I can't hear you.	*Denwa ga tohkutay, kikoe-nikui-n des-ga.* 電話が遠くて、聞えにくいんですが。
Excuse me, I don't speak Japanese.	*Sumimasen-ga, Nihon-go ga wakari-masen.* すみませんが、日本語が分かりません。
Is...there please?	*... san iras-sha-i-mas-ka?* …さんいらっしゃいますか?
Is there anybody who speaks English?	*Aygo ga dekiru shto iras-sha-i-mas-ka?* 英語が出来る人いらっしゃいますか?
Extension..., please.	*Nai-sen ...ban o onegai shimas.* 内線…番をお願いします。
Could you ask him/her to call me back?	*Ato de kakay-naos-yoh onegai shimas.* 後で掛け直すようお願いします。
My name's... My number's...	*Watashi wa ... des.* *Watashi no denwa-bangoh wa ... des.* 私は…です。私の電話番号は…です。
Could you tell him/her I called?	*Watashi kara denwa ga atta-to tsuta-etay kuda-sai.* 私から電話があったと伝えてください。
I'll call back tomorrow.	*Ashta mata denwa o shimas.* 明日また電話をします。

電話です。 There's a phone call for you.
最初に0を押してしてください。 You have to dial '0' first.
ちょっと待ってください。 One moment, please.

通じません。 There's no answer.
話し中です。 The line's busy.
番号が違っています。 You have the wrong number.
ただ今留守です。 He's/she's not here right now.
…時に戻ります。 He'll/she'll be back at…

9.3 Internet/email/social media

The easiest way to stay connected to the Internet in Japan is to rent a portable Wi-Fi router either from your home country or online and have it delivered to your hotel when you reach Japan. Otherwise, download apps like Travel Japan Wi-Fi and Free Wi-Fi Passport to be able to tap into the wide (200,000 to 400,000) range of hotspots around the country after registration. Starbucks, some department stores, train stations and Denny's also offer free Wi-Fi. Another option is to visit a multi-story Internet Café or Manga Kissa, which usually has a collection of manga, Wi-Fi, console games and online gaming computers, snacks, drinks and even showers.

Did you receive my email?	*Watashi no may-ru wa todoki mashta-ka?* 私のメールは届きましたか?
I'd like to send an email.	*May-ru o sohsin shi-tai no des-ga.* メールを送信したいのですが。
I'd like to access my email, can I do it on this computer?	*May-ru o chekk shi-tai no des-ga, kono kompyootah de dekimas-ka?* メールをチェックしたいのですが、このコンピューターで出来ますか?
Could you show me how to log on?	*Rogu-on no shikata o oshie-tay kure-masen-ka?* ログオンの仕方を教えてくれませんか?
Is there an Internet café around here?	*Kono hen ni Intah-netto kafe wa arimas-ka?* このへんにインターネットカフェはありますか?
I cannot get online. Do you have Wi-Fi here?	*Intah-netto ni tsunagari-masen. Muse-ran/wai-fai ga arimas-ka?* インターネットに繋がりません。無線LAN/Wi-Fi がありますか?

What is the network name?	*Netto-wahku-may wa nan des-ka?* ネットワーク名は何ですか?
What is the password?	*Pasu-wahdo wa nan des-ka?* パスワードは何ですか?
I updated my blog.	*Burogu o kohsin shimashta.* ブログを更新しました。
Which browser do you usually use?	*Dono burauza o tsukat-tay imas-ka?* どのブラウザを使っていますか?
Can we become friends on Facebook?	*Feisu-bukku de tomodachi ni nari-masen-ka?* フェイスブックで友達になりませんか?
What is your Facebook ID?	*Feisu-bukku no aidee wa nan des-ka?* フェイスブックのIDは何ですか?
Do you use Twitter/Instagram/Pinterest?	*Tsuit-tah/Instaguramu/Pintarest o yat-tay-imas-ka?* ツイッター／インスタグラム／ピンタレストをやっていますか?
What is your Twitter Instagram/Pinterest handle (username)?	*Tsuit-tah/Instaguramu/Pintarest no yoozah-may wa nan des-ka?* ツイッター／インスタグラム／ピンタレストのユーザー名は何ですか?
Do you tweet often?	*Yoku tsuit-tah de tsubuyaki-mas-ka?* よくツイッターでつぶやきますか?
Can I follow you on Twitter/Instagram/Pinterest?	*Tsuit-tah/Instaguramu/Pintarest de foroh shtay-mo ee des-ka?* ツイッター／インスタグラム／ピンタレストでフォローしてもいいですか?
No, I am not busy. I am just surfing the web for now.	*Ee-ye, isogashku-arimasen-yo. Tada Intah-netto o shtayru-dake des-kara.* いいえ、忙しくありませんよ。ただインターネットをしてるだけですから。
Please help us take a picture.	*Shashin o tot-tay kuda-saimas-ka?/Itadakemas-ka?* 写真を撮ってくださいますか?／いただけますか?
Let's take a selfie.	*Serufee shimasho!* セルフィーしましょう!

I will send you the picture via Whatsapp/Line. What's your mobile number?

Whatsapp/Line de shashin o okurimas. Kay-tai denwa no bangoh wa?
Whatsapp/Lineで写真を送ります。携帯電話の番号は？

Can I charge my phone here?

Koko de kay-tai denwa o joo-den dekimas-ka?
ここで携帯電話を充電できますか？

Can I rent a pocket Wi-Fi router?

Poketto wai-fai o kariraremas-ka?
ポケットWi-Fiを借りられますか？

Can I buy a...

... o kaemas-ka? ……を買えますか？

Can I buy a SIM card?

Sim kahdo o kaemas-ka?
SIM カードを買えますか？

Can I buy a portable charger?

Pohtaburu joo-den-ki o kaemas-ka?
ポータブル充電器を買えますか？

Do you have a printer here?

Koko ni purintah wa arimas-ka?
ここにプリンターはありますか？

How much does it cost to print one sheet of paper?

Insats wa ichi-mai ikura des-ka?
印刷は一枚いくらですか？

Can I put our picture on Facebook/Instagram?

Feisu-bukku/Instaguramu de gazoh o appu dekimas-ka?
フェイスブック／インスタグラムで画像をアップ出来ますか？

Internet ***Intah-netto*** インターネット	smartphone ***sumahto-fon/sumaho*** スマートフォン／スマホ	tweet ***tsueeto/tsubuyaki*** ツイート/つぶやき
email ***ee-may-ru*** Eメール	e-book ***denshi shosheki/ee-bukku*** 電子書籍／イーブック	adapter ***adaputah*** アダプター
texting ***may-ru*** メール	tablet PC ***taburetto-gata pasokon*** タブレット型パソコン	charger ***joo-den-ki*** 充電器
hotspot ***hotto supotto*** ホットスポット	cloud computing ***kuraudo*** クラウド	log-in page ***rogu-in peh-ji*** ログインページ

username
yoo-zah-may
ユーザー名

password
pasu-wahdo
パスワード

software
sofuto-uea
ソフトウェア

web site
uebu-saito
ウェブサイト

browser
burauza
ブラウザ

Wi-Fi
musen ran/wai-fai
無線LAN／Wi-Fi

search engine
sahchi-enjin
サーチエンジン

social networking
sohsharu netto-wahkingu
ソーシャル・ネットワーキング

log on
rogu-on
ログオン

mobile banking
mobairu-bankingu
モバイルバンキング

app/application
apuri/apuri-kayshon
アプリ／
アプリケーション

Wi-Fi built-in digital camera
wai-fai tohsai dejikame
Wi-Fi搭載デジカメ

developer
(sofutouea) kaihatsu-sha
(ソフトウェア)開発者

virus
uirusu
ウィルス

log off
rogu-ofu
ログオフ

malware
maru-uea
マルウェア

laptop
rap-pu top-pu
ラップトップ

hacker
hakkah
ハッカー

@
atto-mahku
アットマーク

dot
dotto
ドット

Do you have this...app?	... no apuri mot-tay mas-ka? ...のアプリ持ってますか?
Do you have this beauty app?	Utsuku-shee no apuri mot-tay mas-ka? 美しいのアプリ持ってますか?
Do you have this mobile game app?	Gehmu no apuri mot-tay mas-ka? ゲームのアプリ持ってますか?
Do you have this subway app?	Chika-tets no apuri mot-tay mas-ka? 地くだ鉄のアプリ持ってますか?
Do you have this train app?	Densha no apuri mot-tay mas-ka? 電車 のアプリ持ってますか?

10. Shopping

Shops usually open around 10am and close around 6pm. Department stores close between 6pm and 9pm, depending on the store and the day. All shops close one day each week. Neighborhood shops, with the exception of supermarkets, tend to close on Sundays. Large department stores are always open on Saturdays and Sundays. 24h convenience stores or *kombini* can now be found in most city areas. Discount stores offer mainstream goods at up to 40% cheaper than other stores. There is a sales tax on all items; this is added to the final bill and is not included in the price displayed. Bargaining is not the norm in Japan, and attempts to do so will generally be met by a flat refusal. In some shops it is okay to ask for a discount when purchasing multiple items. Hundred yen shops like Daiso are found everywhere in Japan, where most things cost just 100 yen. It is customary for shop assistants to greet customers with *irasshaimase* (welcome).

department store *depahto* デパート	100-yen store *hyak-kin* 百均	bicycle repairs/shop *jitensha-ya* 自転車屋
electronics shop/ electrical appliances *denki-ya/denki-ten* 電気屋／電気店	coffee house/café *kis-saten* 喫茶店	supermarket *soo-pah* スーパー
household goods *zakka-ya* 雑貨屋	greengrocer *yaoya* 八百屋	shop *mise* 店
sports shop *supohts yohin-ten* スポーツ用品店	fruit shop *kudamono-ya* 果物屋	second-hand goods *kobutsu-shoh* 古物商

liquor shop
saka-ya
酒屋

shoe shop
kutsu-ya
靴屋

butcher
niku-ya
肉屋

antiques
kot-toh-ten/anteeku
骨董店／アンティーク

shopping arcade
shohten-gai
商店街

food shop
shokuryoh-hin-ten
食料品店

cake shop
kehki-ya
ケーキ屋

tobacconist
tabako-ya
タバコ屋

pharmacist
yak-kyoku
薬局

hardware shop
kanamono-ya
金物屋

kiosk
kiosuku/baiten
キオスク／売店

perfume shop
kohswee-ten
香水店

cosplay shop
kosupure-shoppu
コスプレショップ

jeweler
**kikinzoku-ten/
hohseki-ten**
貴金属店／宝石店

toy shop
omocha-ya
おもちゃ屋

florist
hana-ya
花屋

launderette
koin-randoree
コインランドリー

bookshop
hon-ya
本屋

market
ichiba/mahketto
市場／マーケット

optician
megane-ya
眼鏡屋

bakery
pan-ya
パン屋

beauty parlor
miyoh-in
美容院

hairdresser
toko-ya
床屋

flea market
nomi-no-ichi
のみの市

anime/game store
anime-gehm shoppu
アニメ・ゲームショ
ップ

clothes shop
yoh-hin-ten
洋品店

candy shop
okashi-ya
お菓子屋

hardware store
hohm-sentah
ホームセンター

dry cleaner
kuree-ningu-ya
クリーニング屋

delicatessen
**sohzai-ya/derika-
tessen**
総菜屋／デリカテッ
セン

convenience store
kombini
コンビニ

used bookstore
furuhon-ya
古本屋

souvenir shop
miyagemono-ten
みやげ物店

health food shop
**kenkoh shokuryoh-
hin-ten**
健康食料品店

maid café
may-do kafe
メイドカフェ

10.1 Shopping conversations

Where can I get a jacket?	*Jaketto wa doko de ka-e-mas-ka?* ジャケットはどこで買えますか？
When does this shop open?	*Kono mise wa its akimas-ka?* この店はいつ開きますか？
Could you help me, please? I'm looking for a dress.	*Sumimasen, dores ga hoshee-n des-ga?* すみません、ドレスがほしいんですが？
Could you tell me where the shoe department is?	*Kuts uriba wa doko des-ka?* 靴売場はどこですか？
Do you sell English newspapers?	*Aygo no shimbun wa arimas-ka?* 英語の新聞はありますか？
I'm just looking.	*Chotto mite-iru dakay des.* ちょっと見ているだけです。
I'd also like a shirt.	*Shats mo kuda-sai.* シャツもください。
Could you show me...?	*... o misetay kuda-sai.* …を見せてください。
Do you have something less expensive?	*Motto yaswee no wa arimasen-ka?* もっと安いのはありませんか？
Do you have something smaller?	*Motto chee-sai no wa arimasen-ka?* もっと小さいのはありませんか？
Do you have something larger?	*Motto oh-kee no wa arimasen-ka?* もっと大きいのはありませんか？
I'll take this one.	*Koray kuda-sai.* これください。
Does it come with instructions?	*Setsumay-sho wa hait-tay imas-ka?* 説明書は入っていますか？
It's too expensive.	*Chotto taka-sugimas.* ちょっと高過ぎます。
Could you keep this for me? I'll come back for it later.	*Azukat-tay kuda-sai-masen-ka? Ato de tori ni kimas.* あずかってくださいませんか？ あとで取りに来ます。
Have you got a bag for me, please?	*Tesagay-bukuro arimas-ka?* てさげ袋ありますか？

Could you gift wrap it, please?	*Prezento des-kara, ts-tsu-n-de kuda-sai.* プレゼントですから、包んでください。
I don't need a bag.	*Fukuro wa iri-masen.* 袋はいりません。
Can I have a receipt?	*Re-shee-to o morae mas-ka?* レシートをもらえますか?

すみませんが、ありません。 I'm sorry, we don't have that.
すみませんが、売切れです。 I'm sorry, we're sold out.
レジでお支払いください。 You can pay at the cash desk.
クレジットカードは使えません。 We don't accept credit cards.
外貨は使えません。 We don't accept foreign currency.

10.2 Food

I'd like a hundred grams of chicken, please.	*Tori-niku o hyaku-gram onegai shimas.* 鶏肉を100グラムお願いします。
I'd like five hundred grams of beef, please.	*Gyoo-niku o gohyaku-gram onegai shimas.* 牛肉を500グラムお願いします。
I'd like a kilo of pork, please.	*Buta-niku o ichi-kiro onegai shimas.* 豚肉を1キロお願いします。
Could you slice it/chop it for me, please?	*Usuku/sai-no-may ni kit-tay kuda-sai.* 薄く／さいの目に切ってください。
Could you grate it for me, please?	*Oroshtay kuda-sai.* おろしてください。
Can I order it?	*Choomon dekimas-ka?* 注文出来ますか?
I'll pick it up tomorrow/at...	*Ashta/... ji ni tori ni kimas.* あした／…時に取りに来ます。
Can you eat this?	*Tabemono des-ka?* 食べ物ですか?
Can you drink this?	*Nomimono des-ka?* 飲み物ですか?
What's in it?	*Zai-ryoh wa nan des-ka?* 材料は何ですか?

10.3 Clothing and shoes

I'd like something to go with this.	*Nani-ka kore ni ni-au no ga hoshee-n des-ga.* 何かこれに似合うのがほしいんですが。
Do you have shoes to match this?	*Kore ni ni-au kuts ga arimas-ka?* これに似合う靴がありますか?
I'm a size...in the U.S.	*Amerika no ... saiz nan des-ga.* アメリカの…サイズなんですが。
Can I try this on?	*Shi-chaku dekimas-ka?* 試着出来ますか?
Where's the fitting room?	*Shi-chaku-shits wa doko des-ka?* 試着室はどこですか?
It doesn't fit.	*Kono saiz wa ai-masen.* このサイズは合いません。
This is the right size.	*Kono saiz wa choh-do ee des.* このサイズはちょうどいいです。
It doesn't suit me.	*Ni-ai-masen.* 似合いません。
It's not very comfortable.	*Kigokochi ga yoku arimasen.* 着心地が良くありません。
The heel's too high.	*Kakato ga taka-sugimas.* かかとが高過ぎます。
The heel's too low.	*Kakato ga hiku-sugimas.* かかとが低過ぎます。
Is this/are these genuine leather?	*Kore wa hontoh no kawa des-ka?* これは本当の皮ですか?
I'm looking for a dress for a three-year-old child.	*San-sai no kodomo ni dores ga hoshee-n des-ga.* 3歳の子供にドレスがほしいんですが。
I'd like a silk dress.	*Kinu no dores onegai shimas.* 絹のドレスお願いします。
I'd like a cotton shirt.	*Momen no shats onegaishimas.* 木綿のシャツお願いします。
I'd like a woolen sweater.	*Wooru no sehtah onegaishimas.* ウールのセーターお願いします。
I'd like a linen jacket.	*Asa no jaketto onegaishimas.* 麻のジャケットお願いします。

What temperature can I wash it at?	*Sentaku ondo wa nan-do des-ka?* 洗濯温度は何度ですか?
Will it shrink in the wash?	*Arat-tara, chijimi-mas-ka?* 洗ったら、縮みますか?

Drip dry, please.
Nureta mama hoshtay, kuda-sai.
濡れたまま干してください。

Machine wash
Sentaku-ki de araemas
洗濯機で洗えます

Dry clean, please.
Dorai-kuree-ningu shtay kuda-sai.
ドライクリーニングしてください。

Hand wash, please.
Te de arat-tay kuda-sai.
手で洗ってください。

Do not iron, please.
Airon o kake-naide kuda-sai.
アイロンをかけないでください。

At the cobbler

Could you mend these shoes?	*Kono kuts o shoori dekimas-ka?* この靴を修理出来ますか?
Could you put new soles on these?	*Atara-shee kuts-zoko o tskut-tay kuda-sai.* 新しい靴底を作ってください。
Could you put new heels on these?	*Atara-shee kakato o tskut-tay kuda-sai.* 新しいかかとを作ってください。
When will they be ready?	*Its dekimas-ka?* いつできますか?
I'd like a tin of shoe polish, please.	*Kuts-kreem onegai shimas.* 靴クリームお願いします。
I'd like a pair of shoelaces, please.	*Kutsu-himo onegai shimas.* 靴ひもお願いします。

10.4 Cameras

single-lens reflex (SLR) camera	photo-editing	SD card
ichigan refu-kamera 一眼レフカメラ	*gazoh-shori* 画像処理	*esu-dee (SD) kahdo* SDカード

digital camera **deji-kame** デジカメ	optical zoom **kohgaku zoomu** 光学ズーム	camera shake correction feature **tebure-hosei-kinoh** 手ぶれ補正機能
digital single-lens reflex camera **dejitaru ichigan-refu** デジタル一眼レフ	video **dohga** 動画	high-definition- digital camera **koh-gashits deji- kame** 高画質デジカメ
facial-recognition camera **kao-ninshiki kamera** 顔認識カメラ	pixel **gaso** 画素	

I'd like to print out photos from my digital camera. Where can I do it?
Deji-kame no shashin o insats shi-tai-n des-ga, doko de dekimas-ka?
デジカメの写真を印刷したいんですが、どこで出来ますか?

Can you upload your photos to Facebook?
Shashin o Feisu-bukku ni appu-rohdo shtay kure-masen-ka?
写真をフェイスブックにアップロードしてくれませんか?

I'd like batteries for this digital camera.
Kono kamera ni firum o iretay kuda-sai.
このカメラにフィルムを入れてください。

Two AA batteries, please.
Firum o tori-dashtay kuda-sai.
フィルムを取り出してください。

Can you put in the batteries for me, please?
Batteree o tori-kae nakereba-nari-masen-ka?
バッテリーを取り換えなければなりませんか?

The...is broken.
... ga koware-mashta. …がこわれました。

Could you have a look at my camera, please? It's not working.
Kono kamera o mitay kure-masen-ka? Tsuka-e-naku-nat-tay shimai-mashta.
このカメラを見てくれませんか?使えなくなってしまいました。

Please scan the document and email it to me.
Bunsho o sukyan-shtay may-ru-shtay kuda-sai.
文書をスキャンしてメールしてください。

The flash isn't working.	*Furash ga tentoh shimasen* フラッシュが点灯しません。
My computer ran out of battery.	*Kom-pyoo-tah no bat-teree ga nakunari-mashta.* コンピューターのバッテリーがなくなりました。
I need to change the memory card.	*Memoree kahdo o torikaetai des.* メモリーカードを取り替えたいです。
This computer has a hardware problem.	*Hahdo-uea ni mondai ga arimas.* ハードウェアに問題があります。
This computer has a software problem.	*Sofuto-uea ni mondai ga arimas.* ソフトウェア問題があります。
Does this game have English subtitles?	*Kono gehm ni Aygo no jimaku-ga arimas-ka?* このゲームに英語の字幕がありますか?
Will I be able to play this game on my PS4 in America?	*Amerika no PS4 de kono gaym o suru koto ga dekimas-ka?* アメリカのPS4でこのゲームをすることができますか?
Can I play this game on my XBOX One S in America?	*Amerika no Ekks-bokks Wan Esu de kono gaym o suru koto ga dekimas-ka?* アメリカのXBOX(エックスボックス)ワン-エスでこのゲームをすることができますか?
Can I play this game on my Nintendo Wii in America?	*Amerika no Nintendoh wee de kono gaym o suru koto ga dekimas-ka?* アメリカのニンテンドーWiiでこのゲームをすることができますか?
Can I play this game on my Macbook Air in America?	*Amerika no Makku-bukku ea de kono gaym o suru koto ga dekimas-ka?* アメリカのマックブックエアでこのゲームをすることができますか?

Printing and Processing

| I'd like to have these pictures printed, please. | *Kono firum o genzoh shtay kuda-sai.*
このフィルムを現像してください。 |

I'd like glossy prints for each picture.	*Kono nega o kohtaku no aru mai-zuts print shtay kuda-sai.* このネガを光沢のある枚ずつプリントしてください。
I'd like matte prints for each picture.	*Kono nega o kohtaku no nai mai-zuts print shtay kuda-sai.* このネガを光沢のない枚ずつプリントしてください。
I'd like to have this photo enlarged.	*Kore o hiki-nobashtay kuda-sai.* これを引き伸ばしてください。
How much is processing?	*Genzoh wa ikura des-ka?* 現像はいくらですか?
How much is printing?	*Purinto wa ikura des-ka?* プリントはいくらですか?
How much is the enlargement?	*Hiki-nobashi wa ikura des-ka?* 引き伸ばしはいくらですか?
When will they be ready?	*Its dekimas-ka?* いつできますか?

10.5 At the hairdresser or barber

Do I have to make an appointment?	*Yoyak shi-nakereba nari-masen-ka?* 予約しなければなりませんか?
How long will I have to wait?	*Dono gurai machimas-ka?* どのぐらい待ちますか?
I'd like a shampoo.	*Kami o arat-tay kuda-sai.* 髪を洗ってください。
I'd like a haircut.	*Kami o kit-tay kuda-sai.* 髪を切ってください。
I'd like a shampoo for oily hair please.	*Aburap-poi kami yoh no shampoo onegai shimas.* あぶらっぽい髪用のシャンプーお願いします。
I'd like a shampoo for dry hair please.	*Kansoh shita kami yoh no shampoo onegai shimas.* 乾燥した髪用のシャンプーお願いします。

I'd like a shampoo for permed hair please.	*Pahma o kaketa kami no shampoo onegai shimas.* パーマをかけた髪用のシャンプーお願いします。
I'd like a shampoo for colored hair.	*Someta kami no shampoo onegai shimas.* 染めた髪用のシャンプーお願いします。
I'd like an anti-dandruff shampoo.	*Fu-kay bohshi-yoh no shampoo onegai shimas.* ふけ防止用のシャンプーお願いします。
I'd like a color rinse shampoo.	*Karah shampoo onegai shimas.* カラーシャンプーお願いします。
I want to keep it the same color.	*Kono iro-to onaji ni shtay kuda-sai.* この色と同じにしてください。
I'd like it darker.	*Motto kuroku shtay kuda-sai.* もっと黒くしてください。
I'd like it lighter.	*Motto akaruku shtay kuda-sai.* もっと明るくしてください。
I'd like gel, please.	*Jeru o kaketay kuda-sai.* ジェルをかけてください。
I don't want hair spray.	*He-a spray wa shi-nai de kuda-sai.* ヘアスプレーはしないでください。
I don't want lotion.	*Rohshon wa shi-nai de kuda-sai.* ローション はしないでください。
I'd like short bangs.	*Ma-e-gami o miji-kaku kit-tay kuda-sai.* 前髪を短く切ってください。
Not too short at the back	*Ushiro wa mijika-sugi-nai yoh-ni.* 後は短過ぎないように。
Not too long here	*Koko wa naga-sugi-nai yoh-ni.* ここは長過ぎないように。
It needs a little taken off.	*Skoshi dakay kit-tay kuda-sai.* 少しだけ切ってください。
I want a completely different style.	*Hoka no kamigata ni shi-tai-n des.* 他の髪型にしたいんです。
Please thin my hair a little bit.	*Kami o sukoshi swee-te kuda-sai.* 髪を少しすいてください。

I'd like it the same as that lady's.	*Ano kata no yoh-na kami-gata ni shi-tai-n des-ga.* あの方のような髪型にしたいんですが。
I'd like it the same as in this photo.	*Kono shashin no yoh-na kami-gata ni shi-tai-n des-ga.* この写真のような髪型にしたいんですが。
Could you turn the drier up a bit?	*Draiyah o takaku shtay kuda-sai.* ドライヤーを高くしてください。
Could you turn the drier down a bit?	*Draiyah o hikuku shtay kuda-sai.* ドライヤーを低くしてください。
I'd like a manicure.	*Manikyua o shtay kuda-sai.* マニキュアをしてください。
I'd like a massage.	*Mas-sahji o shtay kuda-sai.* マッサージをしてください。

どんな髪型がいいですか?	What style did you have in mind?
どんな色がいいですか?	What color did you want it?
温度はよろしいですか?	Is the temperature all right for you?
雑誌をお読みになりますか?	Would you like something to read?
何かお飲みになりますか?	Would you like a drink?
これでよろしいですか?	Is this what you had in mind?

Could you trim my bangs?	*Ma-e-gami o kiri-soroetay kuda-sai.* 前髪を切りそろえてください。
Could you trim my beard?	*Higay o kiri-soroetay kuda-sai.* ひげを切りそろえてください。
Could you trim my moustache?	*Kuchi-higay o kiri-soroetay kuda-sai.* 口ひげを切りそろえてください。
I'd like a shave, please.	*Hige o sot-tay kuda-sai.* ひげを剃ってください。
I'd like a wet shave, please.	*Hige-sori-yoh kamisori de sot-tay kuda-sai.* ひげ剃り用カミソリで剃ってください。

11. Tourist Activities

Most airports and train stations in major cities have tourist information counters with English-speaking staff. Look for the map signboards and locate the tourist information counter or office on the map. Otherwise, go to http://jnto.go.jp/eng/arrange/essential to find the number for the tourist information center in your city. Use your Japanese SIM card to call the number, e.g., 03-3841-2871 for the TOBU Sightseeing Service Center at Asakusa Station or call NTT East Information at 0120 364 463 for English-language assistance.

11.1 Places of interest

Most museums, tourist sites, nationally famous temples and gardens charge entrance fees, which average around 400–600 yen for adults. If possible, wear shoes that can be taken off easily, since many tourist attractions, particularly temples and old buildings, require shoes to be removed at the entrance.

Meiji shrine *Meiji jingoo* 明治神宮	Mount Fuji *Fujisan* 富士山	Senso-ji, Asakusa Kannon Temple *Senso-ji/Asakusa Kan'non* 浅草寺／浅草観音
The Golden Pavilion *Kinkaku-ji* 金閣寺	Universal Studios Japan *Yunibahsaru Sutajio Japan* ユニバーサル・スタジ オ・ジャパン	Tokyo Skytree *Tokyo Skai-tsuree* 東京スカイツリー
museum *hakubutsu-kan* 観光案内所		

Tourist Information Center	Hiroshima Peace Memorial	Osaka Castle
Kankoh an-nai-sho	*Hiroshima Heiwa*	*Osaka-jo*
観光案内所	*Kinen-kan*	大阪城
	広島平和記念館	baseball stadium
		yakyoo-joo
		球場

Where's the Tourist Information Center, please?	*Kankoh an-nai-sho wa doko des-ka?* 観光案内所はどこですか？
Do you have a city map?	*Machi no chizu wa arimas-ka?* 町の地図はありますか？
Could you give me some information about...?	*... ni tsu-itay oshie-tay kuda-sai.* …について教えてください。
How much is that?	*Ikura des-ka?* いくらですか？
What are the main places of interest?	*Omo ni doko ga omoshiro-i des-ka?* 主にどこが面白いですか？
Could you point them out on the map?	*Chizu de oshetay kuda-sai.* 地図で教えてください。
What do you recommend?	*Nani-ka osusume wa?* 何かおすすめは？
We'll be here for a few hours.	*Koko ni ni-san jikan imas.* ここに二、三時間います。
We'll be here for a day.	*Koko ni ichi-nichi imas.* ここに一日います。
We'll be here for a week.	*Koko ni is-shoo-kan imas.* ここに一週間います。
We're interested in...	*... ni kyohmi ga arimas-ga.* …に興味がありますが。
Is there a scenic walk around the city?	*Shinai kankoh wa arimas-ka?* 市内観光はありますか？
How long does it take?	*Dono gurai jikan ga kakarimas-ka?* どのぐらい時間がかかりますか？
Where does it start?	*Shuppats-ten wa doko des-ka?* 出発点はどこですか？

Where does it end?	*Shooten wa doko des-ka?* 終点はどこですか?
Are there any boat cruises here?	*Yooran-sen ga arimas-ka?* 遊覧船がありますか?
Where can we board?	*Doko de fune ni noremas-ka?* どこで船に乗れますか?
Are there any bus tours?	*Kankoh bas ga arimas-ka?* 観光バスがありますか?
Where do we get on?	*Doko de bas ni noremas-ka?* どこでバスに乗れますか?
Is there a guide who speaks English?	*Aygo no gaid ga imas-ka?* 英語のガイドがいますか?
What trips can we take around the area?	*Doko-ka tanoshee shoh-ryokoh wa arimas-ka?* どこか楽しい小旅行はありますか?
Are there any excursions?	*Kankoh-tsuah ga arimas-ka?* 観光ツアーがありますか?
Where do they go to?	*Doko-e ikimas-ka?* どこへ行きますか?
We'd like to go to...	*... e ikitai-n des-ga.* …へ行きたいんですが。
How long is the trip?	*Tsuah wa nan-jikan kakarimas-ka?* ツアーは何時間かかりますか?
How long do we stay in...?	*... ni wa dono kurai tai-zai shimas-ka?* …にはどのくらい滞在しますか?
Are there any guided tours?	*Gaid-tski-tsuah ga arimas-ka?* ガイド付きツアーがありますか?
How much free time will we have there?	*Dono-gurai jiyoo jikan ga arimas-ka?* どのぐらい自由時間がありますか?
We want to go hiking.	*Haiking ni iki-tai-n des-ga.* ハイキングに行きたいんですが。
Can we hire a guide?	*Gaid o tanomemas-ka?* ガイドをたのめますか?

Can I book mountain huts?	*Yama-goya no yoyaku ga dekimas-ka?* 山小屋の予約が出来ますか?
What time does...open?	*Nan-ji ni ... ga akimas-ka?* 何時に…が開きますか?
What time does...close?	*Nan-ji ni ... ga shimarimas-ka?* 何時に…が閉まりますか?
What days is...open?	*Nan-yohbi ni ... ga ai-tay imas-ka?* 何曜日に…が開いていますか?
What days is...closed?	*Nan-yohbi ni ... ga shimat-tay imas-ka?* 何曜日に…が閉まっていますか?
What's the admission price?	*Nyoojoh-ryoh wa ikura des-ka?* 入場料はいくらですか?
Is there a discount for a group?	*Groop no waribiki kippu arimas-ka?* グループの割引切符ありますか?
Is there a discount for students?	*Gaksay no waribiki kippu arimas-ka?* 学生の割引切符ありますか?
Is there a discount for children?	*Kodomo no waribiki kippu arimas-ka?* 子供の割引切符ありますか?
Is there a discount for seniors?	*Rokujoo-go-sai i-joh no waribiki kippu arimas-ka?* 65歳以上の割引切符ありますか?
Can I film here?	*Satsu-ay shtay mo ee des-ka?* 撮影してもいいですか?
Can I take (flash) photos?	*(frash-de) Shashin o tot-tay mo ee des-ka?* (フラッシュで) 写真を撮ってもいいですか?
Do you have any postcards of...?	*... no e-hagaki ga arimas-ka?* …の絵葉書がありますか?
Do you have an English catalogue?	*Aygo no katarog arimas-ka?* 英語のカタログありますか?
Do you have an English program?	*Aygo no program arimas-ka?* 英語のプログラムありますか?
Do you have an English brochure?	*Aygo no panf-retto arimas-ka?* 英語のパンフレットありますか?

11.2 Going out

Pick up an English language newspapers or a free visitors' guide from your hotel for information about entertainment options in the area, such as movies, theatrical performances etc. You can also use the Teletourist service in Tokyo or go online to look for these events. Evening dress is rarely worn to the theater. Shows start early, usually at 6.30pm or 7pm. Traditional theater includes *Kabuki, No,* and *Bunraku*. Films are generally shown in the language of origin with Japanese subtitles.

Do you have this week's entertainment guide?	*Kon-shoo no program wa arimas-ka?* 今週のプログラムはありますか?
Do you have this month's entertainment guide?	*Kon-gets no program wa arimas-ka?* 今月のプログラムはありますか?
What's on tonight?	*Kom-ban no program wa?* 今晩のプログラムは?
We want to go to...	*... ni ikitai-n des-ga.* …に行きたいんですが。
Which films are showing?	*Donna ayga ga arimas-ka?* どんな映画がありますか?
What sort of film is that?	*Dono yoh-na ayga des-ka?* どのような映画ですか?
It's an adult (over 18) film.	*Sore wa sayjin ayga des.* それは成人映画です。
It's the original version of the movie.	*Sore wa orijinaru-ban no ayga des.* それはオリジナル版の映画です。
The movie has English subtitles.	*Sore wa jimaku-tski no ayga des.* それは字幕付きの映画です。
It's dubbed.	*Sore wa fuki-kae no ayga des.* それは吹替の映画です。
Is it a continuous showing?	*Kuri-keashi joh-en shimas-ka?* 繰り返し上演しますか?
What's on at the theater?	*Nani-ka ee show wa arimas-ka?* 何かいいショーはありますか?

What's on at the concert hall?	*Nani-ka ee konsah-to hoh-ru wa arimas-ka?* 何かいい コンサートホールはありますか？
What's on at the opera?	*Nani-ka ee opera wa arimas-ka?* 何かいいオペラはありますか？
Where can I find a good disco around here?	*Kono-hen ni ee disko wa arimas-ka?* この辺にいいディスコはありますか？
Is it members only?	*Kai-in dakay des-ka?* 会員だけですか？
Where can I find a good nightclub around here?	*Kono-hen ni ee naito-krab wa arimas-ka?* この辺にいいナイト・クラブはありますか？
What time does the show start?	*Show wa nan-ji kara des-ka?* ショーは何時からですか？
Is there a cover charge for entry to this bar?	*Kono bah wa sahbisu-ryoh ga arimas-ka?* このバーはサービス料がありますか？
Is it Ladies' Night?	*Redeesu naito des-ka?* レディースナイトですか？
What is your recommended drink?	*Osusume no nomimono wa?* おすすめの飲み物は？
Is this All-You-Can Drink?	*Nomi-hohdai des-ka?* 飲み放題ですか？

11.3 Booking tickets

Could you reserve some tickets?	*Chiketto o yoyaku dekimas-ka?* チケットを予約出来ますか？
Could you reserve a seat in the orchestra?	*Ik-kai-seki o yoyaku dekimas-ka?* 一階席を予約出来ますか？
Could you reserve a seat at the balcony?	*Ni-kai-seki o yoyaku dekimas-ka?* 二階席を予約出来ますか？
Could you reserve box seats (for me)?	*Bokks-seki o yoyaku dekimas-ka?* ボックス席を予約出来ますか？
Could you reserve a table at the front?	*Ma-e-no-hoh o yoyaku dekimas-ka?* 前の方を予約出来ますか？

Could you reserve a table in the middle?	*Man'naka o yoyaku dekimas-ka?* 真ん中を予約出来ますか?
Could you reserve a table at the back?	*Ushro-no-hoh o yoyaku dekimas-ka?* 後ろの方を予約出来ますか?
Could I reserve...seats for the...o'clock performance?	*... ji no joh-en no kippu o ... mai yoyaku dekimas-ka?* …時の上演の切符を…枚予約出来ますか?
Are there any seats left for tonight?	*Kom-ban no kippu wa mada arimas-ka?* 今晩の切符はまだありますか?
How much is a ticket?	*Ichi-mai ikura des-ka?* 一枚いくらですか?
When can I pick the tickets up?	*Kippu wa its morae-mas-ka?* 切符はいつもらえますか?
I have a reservation.	*Yoyaku shimashta.* 予約しました。
My name's...	*Watashi wa ... des.* 私は…です。

どの演目に予約したいんですか?
  Which performance would you like to reserve?
どんな座席がほしいんですか? Where would you like to sit?
すみませんが、売切れです。 Everything's sold out.
立ち見席だけ残っています。 It's standing room only.
二階席だけ残っています。 We've only got balcony seats left.
一階席だけ残っています。 We've only got orchestra seats left.
前の座席が残っています。 We've only got seats left at the front.
後の座席が残っています。何枚ですか? We've only got seats
  left at the back. How many seats would you like?
…時までに切符を取りに来なければなりません。
  You'll have to pick up the tickets before...o'clock.
切符を見せてください。 Tickets, please.
こちらの席です。 This is your seat.

12. Sports Activities

The most popular spectator sports are baseball, soccer, and *sumo*. There are no public golf courses, but golf driving ranges are found in most places. Public tennis courts get booked very quickly. Fitness and sports clubs are widespread.

12.1 Sporting questions

mountain climbing **tozan** 登山	yoga **yoga** ヨガ	open-air bath **rotem-buro** 露天風呂
hiking **hai-king** ハイキング	power spots **pawah-suppotto** パワースポット	mixed-baths **kon-yoku** 混浴
forest bathing **shinryin'yoku** 森林浴	hot spring **onsen** 温泉	day-trip hot spring **higaeri onsen** 日帰り温泉
snowboarding **sunoh-bohdo/sunobo** スノーボード／スノボ	baseball **yakyoo** 野球	driving range **gorufu renshoo-joh** ゴルフ練習場
skiing **sukee** スキー	tennis **tenisu** テニス	soccer **sakkah** サッカー

Where can we...around here?	*Kono-hen de ... ga dekimas-ka?* この辺で…が出来ますか？
Can I hire a...here?	*Koko de ... ga kari-rare-mas-ka?* ここで…が借りられますか？

Can I take...lessons?	*... no ressun ga uke-rare-mas-ka?* …のレッスンが受けられますか？
How much is that per hour/day/turn?	*Ichi-jikan/ichi-nichi/ik-kai ikura des-ka?* 一時間／一日／一回いくらですか？
Do I need a permit for that?	*Kyoka-sho ga hits-yoh des-ka?* 許可書が必要ですか？
Where can I get the permit?	*Kyoka-sho wa doko de hak-koh saremas-ka?* 許可書はどこで発行されますか？
My hobby is mountain climbing.	*Watashi no shumi wa tozan des.* 私の趣味は登山です。
Where is a good place to go hiking?	*Haiking o suru nara doko ga ee des-ka?* ハイキングをするならどこがいいですか？
Where is a good place to go mountain climbing?	*Tozan o suru nara doko ga ee des-ka?* 登山をするならどこがいいですか？
Is there a famous "power spot" around here?	*Yoo-may na pawah-supot-to ga kono hen ni arimas-ka?* 有名なパワースポットがこの辺にありますか？
Is there a good hot spring around here?	*Kono hen ni yoi onsen wa arimas-ka?* この辺に良い温泉はありますか？
Which day-trip hot spring is the closest from here?	*Koko kara ichiban chikai higaeri onsen wa doko des-ka?* ここから一番近い日帰り温泉はどこですか？
Where is the open-air bath?	*Rotem-buro wa doko des-ka?* 露天風呂はどこですか？
What are the rules for using the mixed baths?	*Kon-yoku suru toki no kimari wa nan des-ka?* 混浴するときの決まりは何ですか？
Do we have to wear something when going to the mixed baths?	*Kon-yoku suru toki wa, nani-ka kinaito ikemasen-ka?* 混浴するときは、何か着ないといけませんか？

12.2 By the waterfront

Is it a long way to the sea still?	*Kai-gan maday mada toh-i des-ka?* 海岸までまだ遠いですか?
Is there a swimming pool around here?	*Kono hen ni pooru wa arimas-ka?* この辺にプールはありますか?
Is there a sandy beach around here?	*Kono hen ni sunahama wa arimas-ka?* この辺に砂浜はありますか?
Is there mooring around here?	*Kono hen ni fu-toh wa arimas-ka?* この辺に埠頭はありますか?
Are there any rocks here?	*Kono-hen ni iwa ga arimas-ka?* この辺に岩がありますか?
When's high tide?	*Its man-choh des-ka?* いつ満潮ですか?
When's low tide?	*Its kan-choh des-ka?* いつ干潮ですか?
What's the water temperature?	*Swee-on wa nan-do des-ka?* 水温は何度ですか?
Is it very deep here?	*Totemo fu-kai des-ka?* とても深いですか?
Can you stand here?	*Tatemas-ka?* 立てますか?
Is it safe for children to swim here?	*Kodomo-ga anzen ni oyogemas-ka?* 子供が安全に泳げますか?
Are there any currents?	*Nagare wa tsyoi des-ka?* 流れは強いですか?
Are there any rapids in this river?	*Kono kawa ni kyooryoo ga arimas-ka?* この川に急流がありますか?
Are there any waterfalls in this river?	*Kono kawa ni taki ga arimas-ka?* この川に滝がありますか?
What does that flag mean?	*Ano hata wa doh yoo imi des-ka?* あの旗はどういう意味ですか?
What does that buoy mean?	*Ano bui wa doh yoo imi des-ka?* あのブイはどういう意味ですか?
Are there any sea creatures we should be wary of?	*Kinen na um-no-ikimono wa imas-ka?* 危険な海の生き物はいますか?

Are the currents very strong?	*Umi no nagare wa tsyoi des-ka?* 海の流れは強いですか？
Is there a lifeguard on duty?	*Raifu-gahdo wa imas-ka?* ライフガードはいますか？

Fishing water **Tsuri-ba** つり場	Permits only **Yoh-kyoka-sho** 要許可書	No surfing **Sahfin kinshi** サーフィン禁止
Danger **Kiken/chooi** 危険／注意	No swimming **Yoo-ei kinshi** 遊泳禁止	No fishing **Tsuri kinshi** つり禁止

12.3 In the snow

Can I take ski lessons here?	*Koko de skee no ressun ga ukerare-mas-ka?* ここでスキーのレッスンが受けられますか？
– for beginners	*shoshin-sha* 初心者
– for advanced	*joh-kyoo-sha* 上級者
How large are the groups?	*Groop wa nan-nin gurai des-ka?* グループは何人ぐらいですか？
What language are the classes in?	*Nani-go de oshie-raremas-ka?* 何語で教えられますか？
I'd like a lift pass, please.	*Rift no ichi-nichi-ken o kuda-sai.* リフトの一日券をください。
Must I give you a passport photo?	*Shohmay shashin ga irimas-ka?* 証明写真がいりますか？
Where can I have a passport photo taken?	*Doko de shohmay shashin o tot-tay moraemas-ka?* どこで証明写真を撮ってもらえますか？
Where are the beginners' slopes?	*Shoshin-sha no gerenday wa doko des-ka?* 初心者のゲレンデはどこですか？

Are there any trails for cross-country skiing?	*Kono hen de kros-kantree-skee ga dekimas-ka?* この辺でクロスカントリースキーができますか?
Are the ski lifts in operation?	*Skeerift wa ugoitay-imas-ka?* スキーリフトは動いていますか?
Are the chair lifts in operation?	*Rift wa ugoitay-imas-ka?* リフトは動いていますか?
Are the slopes usable?	*Gerenday wa shiyoh dekimas-ka?* ゲレンデは使用出来ますか?
Can we do night skiing?	*Yakan no skee wa dekimas-ka?* 夜間のスキーは出来ますか?
Can I rent the equipment here?	*Skee yoh-hin wa karirare-mas-ka?* スキー用品は借りられますか?
How much will it cost to rent skis?	*Skee wa ikura des-ka?* スキーはいくらですか?
How much will it cost to rent gloves?	*Tebukuro wa ikura des-ka?* 手袋 はいくらですか?
How much will it cost to rent boots?	*Boots wa ikura des-ka?* ブーツはいくらですか?
How much will it cost to rent a ski jacket?	*Skee-uea wa ikura des-ka?* スキーウェアはいくらですか?
Where's the best run for snowboarding?	*Sunoh-bohdo o suru no wa doko ga ichiban ee des-ka?* スノーボードをするのはどこが一番いいですか?
Do you have classes for children?	*Kodomo no skee kyohshits wa arimas-ka?* 子供のスキー教室はありますか?
Will the classes be taught in English?	*Skee kyohshits wa aygo de oshie-tay kuremas-ka?* スキー教室は英語で教えてくれますか?
Can we do snow sledding or tubing?	*Sori ya tai-ya de subette-mo ee des-ka?* ソリやタイヤで滑ってもいいですか?

13. Health Matters

Hospitals or clinics with English-speaking staff can be found in most large cities. Because of the high cost of medical and dental treatment, it is advisable to purchase travel insurance. There are pharmacies in every neighborhood.

13.1 Calling a doctor

Could you call a doctor quickly, please?
Hayaku o-isha-san o yonday kitay kuda-sai.
早くお医者さんを呼んできてください。

Could you get a doctor quickly, please?
Hayaku o-isha-san o tsretay-kitay kuda-sai.
早くお医者さんを連れてきてください。

When is the doctor in the clinic?
O-isha-san no shinsats-jikan wa its des-ka?
お医者さんの診察時間はいつですか?

When can the doctor come?
O-isha-san wa its koremas-ka?
お医者さんはいつ来れますか?

I'd like to make an appointment to see the doctor.
O-isha-san no yoyaku o shtay kuda-sai.
お医者さんの予約をしてください。

I have an appointment to see the doctor at...
Watashi wa ... ji ni o-isha-san ni au yakusoku ga arimas.
私は…時にお医者さんに会う約束があります。

Is there an English-speaking doctor?
Aygo ga hanaseru isha ga arimas-ka?
英語が話せる医者がありますか?

Is there a pharmacist on weekend duty?
Dono yak-kyoku ga shoomats kimmu des-ka?
どの薬局が週末勤務ですか?

13.2 What's wrong?

I don't feel well.	*Gu-ai ga waru-i-n des.* 具合が悪いんです。
I'm dizzy.	*Me-mai ga shimas.* めまいがします。
I'm ill.	*Byohki des.* 病気です。
I'm sick.	*Kibun ga waru-i-n des.* 気分が悪いんです。
I have a cold.	*Kazay des.* 風邪です。
It hurts here.	*Koko ga i-tai-n des.* ここが痛いんです。
I've been throwing up.	*Modoshtay shimatta-n des.* もどしてしまったんです。
I'm running a temperature of...degrees.	*... do no nets ga arimas.* …度の熱があります。
I've been stung by a hornet.	*Suzume-bachi ni sasare-mashta.* スズメバチに刺されました。
I've been stung by an insect.	*Mushi ni sasare-mashta.* 虫 に刺されました。
I've been stung by a jellyfish.	*Kurage ni sasare-mashta.* クラゲに刺されました。
I've been bitten by a dog.	*Inu ni kamare-mashta.* 犬に噛まれました。
I've been bitten by a snake.	*Hebi ni kamare-mashta.* 蛇に噛まれました。
I've been bitten by an animal.	*Dohbuts ni kamare-mashta.* 動物に噛まれました。
I've cut myself.	*Kiri-kizu o tske-mashta.* 切り傷をつけました。
I've burned myself.	*Yakedo o shimashta.* やけどをしました。
I've grazed myself.	*Hada o suri-muki-mashta.* 肌をすりむきました。
I've had a fall.	*Korobi-mashta.* ころびました。

I've sprained my ankle.　*Ashi-kubi o kujiki-mashta.*
足首をくじきました。

I've been feeling nauseous.　*Hakike ga shtay-imas.*
吐き気がしています。

13.3　The consultation

どんな症状ですか?　What seems to be the problem?
その症状はどのぐらい 続いていますか?
　How long have you had these symptoms?
この症状は初めてですか?　Have you had this trouble before?
熱は何度ですか? 脱いでください。How high is your
　temperature? Get undressed, please.
上着を取ってください。　Strip to the waist, please.
あそこで脱いでください。　You can undress there.
左/右腕をまくってください。
　Roll up your left/right sleeve, please.
ここに横になってください。Lie down here, please.
ここが痛いですか?　Does this hurt?
深呼吸してください。　Breathe deeply.
口を開けてください。　Open your mouth.

Patients' medical history

I'm a diabetic.　　　　　*Toh-nyoh-byoh des.* 糖尿病です。

I have a heart condition.　*Shinzoh-byoh des.* 心臓病です。

I have asthma.　　　　　*Zensoku des.* ぜん息です。

I'm allergic to...　　　　*... no arerugee des.* …のアレルギーです。

I have an allergy to　　　*Penicillin no yakuzai arerugee ga arimas.*
　penicillin.　　　　　　ペニシリンの薬剤アレルギーがあり
　　　　　　　　　　　　ます。

I have an allergy to　　　*Amokishishirin no yakuzai arerugee ga*
　amoxicillin.　　　　　*arimas.*
　　　　　　　　　　　　アモキシシリンの薬剤アレルギーがあ
　　　　　　　　　　　　ります。

I'm...months pregnant.	*Ninshin ... kagets des.* 妊娠…ヶ月です。
I'm on a diet.	*Shokuji saygen o shtay imas.* 食事制限をしています。
I'm on medication.	*Kusuri o non-de imas.* 薬を飲んでいます。
I'm on the pill.	*Piru o non-de imas.* ピルを飲んでいます。
I've had a heart attack once before.	*Shinzoh mahi o okoshta koto ga arimas.* 心臓麻痺をおこしたことがあります。
I've had a(n)...operation.	*... no shujuts o uke-mashta.* …の手術を受けました。
I've been ill recently.	*Sai-kin maday byohki deshta.* 最近まで病気でした。
I have an ulcer.	*Kai-yoh ga arimas.* 潰瘍があります。
I have my period.	*Seiri-choo des.* 生理中です。
I've injured my wrist before.	*Ma-e ni tekubi o itame-mashta.* 前に手首を痛めました。
I've injured my ankle before.	*Ma-e ni ashikubi o itame-mashta.* 前に足首を痛めました。
I've injured my knee before.	*Ma-e ni hiza o itame-mashita.* 前に膝を痛めました。

何かに対してアレルギーがありますか?
  Do you have any allergies?
薬を使っていますか? Are you on any medication?
食事制限をしていますか? Are you on a diet?
妊娠中ですか? Are you pregnant?
破傷風の予防接種をしましたか?
  Have you had a tetanus injection?

The diagnosis

深刻なものではありません。 It's nothing serious.
…が骨折しています。 Your ...is broken.
…にあざがあります。 You have a/some bruised...
…をくじいています。 You have (a) torn...
炎症を起こしています。 You have an infection.
虫垂炎を起こしています。 You have appendicitis.
気管支炎を起こしています。 You have bronchitis.
性病です。 You have a venereal disease.
流行性感冒です。 You have the flu.
心臓麻痺を起こしています。 You've had a heart attack.
(ウイルス／バクテリアに) 感染しています。
　You have a (viral.../bacterial...) infection.
肺炎です。 You have pneumonia.
潰瘍があります。 You have an ulcer.
筋をちがえました。 You've pulled a muscle.
腟の感染症です。 You have a vaginal infection.
食中毒です。 You have food poisoning.
日射病です。 You have sunstroke.
…のアレルギーがあります。 You're allergic to ...
妊娠中です。 You're pregnant.
あなたの血液を検査したいです。
　I'd like to have your blood tested.
あなたの小便検査したいです。 I'd like to have your urine tested.
あなたの大便検査したいです。 I'd like to have your stools tested.
傷口を縫い合わせなければなりません。 It needs stitches.
専門医に紹介します。 I'm referring you to a specialist.
病院に紹介します。 I'm sending you to the hospital.
X線写真を撮らなければなりません。
　You'll need to have some X-rays taken.
ちょっと待合室で待っていてください。
　Could you wait in the waiting room, please?
手術が必要です。 You'll need an operation.

Is it contagious?	*Densen-say des-ka?* 伝染性ですか?
How long do I have to stay in bed?	*Dono gu-rai beddo ni inakareba nari-masen-ka?* どのぐらいベッドにいなければなりませんか?
How long do I have to stay in the hospital?	*Dono gu-rai byoh-in ni inakareba nari-masen-ka?* どのぐらい病院にいなければなりませんか?
Do I have to go on a special diet?	*Shokuji saygen o shinakereba nari-masen-ka?* 食事制限をしなければなりませんか?
Am I allowed to travel?	*Ryokoh shtay mo ee des-ka?* 旅行してもいいですか?
When do I have to come back?	*Its ukagawa-nakereba nari-masen-ka?* いつ伺わなければなりませんか?
I'll come back tomorrow.	*Mata ashta ukagai-mas.* また明日伺います。
May I have a receipt for my insurance claims?	*Hoken-yoh no ryohshoo-sho-o moraemas-ka?* 保険用の領収書をもらえますか?
Can I have a copy of the diagnosis for my insurance claims?	*Hokenkin saykyoo no shindansho no utsushi o moraemas-ka?* 保険金請求の診断書の写しをもらえますか?

13.4 Medications and prescriptions

How do I take this medicine?	*Kono kusuri wa donoyoh ni nomimas-ka?* この薬はどのように飲みますか?
How many (pills/drops/ injections/spoonfuls) each time?	*Ik-kai ni dono-kurai-zuts des-ka?* 一回にどのくらいずつですか?
How many times a day?	*Ichi-nichi, nankai des-ka?* 一日、何回ですか?

I've forgotten my medication. At home I take...	*Kusuri o wasuretay shimatta-n des-ga, its-mo wa ... o tskat-tay imas.* 薬を忘れてしまったんですが、いつもは…を使っています。
Could you write a prescription for me?	*Shohoh-sen o dashtay kuda-sai-masen-ka?* 処方箋を出してくださいませんか？
I can't swallow tablets. Do you have that in liquid form?	*Johzai ga nomenai no de, mizu-gusuri o morae-masen-ka?* 錠剤が飲めないので、水薬をもらえませんか？

抗生物質の処方書きます。 I'm prescribing antibiotics.
飲み薬の処方書きます。 I'm prescribing a mixture.
トランキライザーの処方書きます。 I'm prescribing a tranquilizer.
鎮痛剤の処方書きます。 I'm prescribing painkillers.
休まなければなりません。 Have lots of rest.
外へ出かけてはいけません。 Stay indoors.
寝ていなければなりません。 Stay in bed.
明日…日後にここにきてください。 Come back tomorrow.
…日後にここにきてください。 Come back in...days' time.

before meals *shoku-zen ni* 食前に	for...days *...nichi kakan* …日間	not for internal use *gaiyoh nomi* 外用のみ
capsules *kapuseru* カプセル	injections *choosha* 注射	...times a day *ichi-nichi... kai* 一日…回
dissolve in water *mizu ni tokasu* 水に溶かす	ointment *nankoh* 軟膏	finish the prescription *kanchi suru* 完治する

drops	rub on	This medication impairs
tenteki-yaku	***tsukeru***	your driving.
点滴薬	つける	***Kono kusuri wa kuruma***
		no unten ni shishow o
tablets	take	***kitashi-masu.***
johzai	***nomu***	この薬は車の運転に
錠剤	飲む	支障をきたします。
swallow whole,	every...hours	spoonfuls (tablespoons/
please	***...jikan-oki ni***	teaspoons)
zembu nonde kuda-sai	…時間おきに	***supoon (dai/show)***
全部飲んでください		スプーン（大／小）

13

13.5 **At the dentist**

Do you know a good dentist?	***Ee ha-isha o sht-tay imas-ka?*** いい歯医者を知っていますか？
Could you make a dentist's appointment for me?	***Watashi no tame o ha-isha ni yoyaku shtay kuda-sai masen-ka?*** 私のためを歯医者に予約してください ませんか？
It's urgent.	***Isoi-de imas.*** 急いでいます。
Can I come in today, please?	***Kyoh uka-ga-e mas-ka?*** 今日伺えますか？
I have a(terrible) toothache.	***(sugoku) Ha ga i-tai-n des.*** （すごく）歯が痛いんです。
Could you prescribe a painkiller for me?	***Chintsoo-zai o shohoh shtay kuda-sai.*** 鎮痛剤を処方してください
Could you give me a painkiller?	***Chintsoo-zai o kuda-sai.*** 鎮痛剤をください。
A piece of my tooth has broken off.	***Ha ga ore-mashta.*** 歯が折れました。
My filling's come out.	***Ha no tsume-mono ga tore-mashta.*** 歯のつめものがとれました。

I have a broken crown.	*Shikan ga koware-mashta.* 歯冠がこわれました。
I'd like a local anesthetic.	*Kyokusho maswee o kaketay kuda-sai.* 局所麻酔をかけてください。
I don't want a local anaesthetic.	*Kyokusho maswee o kake-nai-de kuda-sai.* 局所麻酔をかけないでください。
Can you do a temporary repair job?	*Ohkyoo shochi o shtay kuda-sai.* 応急処置をしてください。
I don't want this tooth pulled.	*Kono ha wa nuka-nai-day kuda-sai.* この歯は抜かないでください。
My dentures are broken.	*Ireba ga koware-mashta.* 入れ歯がこわれました。
Can you fix them?	*Shoori dekimas-ka?* 修理できますか?

どの歯が痛いんですか? Which tooth hurts?

はれています。 You have an abscess.

歯根の治療が必要です。 I'll have to do a root canal.

この歯にを詰めなければ。 I'll have to fill this tooth.

この歯に抜かなければ。 I'll have to pull this tooth.

この歯をけずらなければなりません。 I'll have to file this tooth down.

穴を開けなければなりません。 I'll have to drill.

口を大きく開けてください。 Open wide, please.

口を閉めてください。 Close your mouth, please.

口をゆすいでください。 Rinse, please.

まだ痛いですか? Does it hurt still?

14. Emergencies

Emergency phone numbers: Police: 110; Ambulance/Fire: 119. On a public phone, press the red button and dial; no money is necessary. Speak slowly and clearly if there is no Japanese speaker with you. If you need English-language assistance or travel information call NTT East Information at 0120 364 463 (including the 0) from your mobile phone (use Skype or a Japanese SIM card to reduce costs).

14.1 Asking for help

Help!	*Tas-ketay!* 助けて！
Fire!	*Kaji!* 火事！
Police!	*Kay-sats!* 警察！
Quick!	*Hayaku!* 早く！
Danger!/Watch Out!	*Abu-nai!* 危ない！
Be careful!	*Ki-o-tsketay!* 気をつけて！
Stop!	*Tomaray!* 止まれ！
Don't!	*Shi-nai-de!* しないで！
Let go!	*Te o hanashtay!* 手をはなして！
Stop that thief!	*Doroboh o tometay!* 泥棒を止めて！
Could you help me, please?	*Chotto, sumimasen.* ちょっと、すみません。
Where's the police station?	*Shohkaki wa doko-des-ka?* 警察署はどこですか？

Where's the emergency exit?	*Hijoh-guchi wa doko-des-ka?* 非常口はどこですか?
Where's the fire escape?	*Hinan-kai-dan wa doko-des-ka?* 避難階段はどこですか?
Where's the fire extinguisher?	*Shohkaki wa doko-des-ka?* 消火器はどこですか?
Call the fire department!	*Shohbohsha o yonday!* 消防車を呼んで!
Call the police!	*Kaysats o yonday!* 警察を呼んで!
Call an ambulance!	*Kyookyoosha o yonday!* 救急車を呼んで!
Where's the nearest phone?	*Denwa wa doko des-ka?* 電話はどこですか?
Could I use your phone?	*Denwa o ts-kawashtay kuda-sai.* 電話を使わせてください。
What's the number for the police?	*Kaysats wa namban des-ka?* 警察は何番ですか?

14.2 Lost items

The railways, subway lines, and taxi companies have lost-and-found services.

I've lost my camera.	*Deji-kame o nakushi-mashta.* デジカメをなくしました。
I've left my cell phone on the train.	*Densha ni kay-tai o wasurete shimai-mashta.* 電車に携帯を忘れてしまいました。
I've lost my purse/wallet.	*Saifu o nakushi-mashta.* 財布をなくしました。
I left my wallet here yesterday.	*Kinoh saifu o koko ni oki-wasure-mashta.* 昨日財布をここに置き忘れました。
I left my mobile phone here.	*Koko ni kay tai o oki-wasure-mashta.* ここに携帯を置き忘れました。
Did you find my camera?	*Watashi no deji-kame wa mitsukari-mashta-ka?* 私のデジカメは見つかりましたか?

It was right here.	*Koko ni arimashta.* ここにありました。
It's quite valuable.	*Totemo kichoh na shina des.* とても貴重な品です。
Where's the lost and found office?	*Wasuremono-gakari wa doko des-ka?* 忘れ物係りはどこですか？

Accidents

Robbery and violent crime are rare in Japan. The police maintain a visible presence through a network of small police stations called *koban*, located at train stations and in most neighborhoods. The policemen will help you find your way if you are lost.

There's been an accident.	*Jiko ga oki-mashta.* 事故が起きました。
Someone's fallen into the water.	*Hito ga mizu ni ochi-mashta.* 人が水に落ちました。
There's a fire.	*Kaji des.* 火事です。
Is anyone hurt?	*Kega o shita hito wa imas-ka?* 怪我をした人はいますか？
Some people have been injured.	*Keganin ga imas.* 怪我人がいます。
No one's been injured.	*Keganin wa imasen.* 怪我人はいません。
There's someone in the car/train still.	*Hito ga mada kuruma/ressha ni nokot-tay imas.* 人がまだ車／列車に残っています。
It's not too bad. Don't worry.	*Sore-hodo demo arimasen. Shimpai shi-nai de kuda-sai.* それほどでもありません。心配しない でください。
Leave everything the way it is, please.	*Nani-mo sawara-nai-day kuda-sai.* 何もさわらないでください。
I want to talk to the police first.	*Mazu kaysats to hanashi-tai-n des.* まず警察と話したいんです。

I want to take a photo first.	*Mazu shashin o tori-tai-n des.* まず写真を撮りたいんです。
Here's my name and address.	*Kore ga watashi no nama-e to joosho des.* これが私の名前と住所です。
Could I have your name and address?	*Anata no nama-e to joosho o oshie-tay kuda-sai.* あなたの名前と住所を教えてください。
Could I see your identification?	*Mibun shohmay-sho o misetay kuda-sai.* 身分証明書を見せてください。
Could I see your insurance papers?	*Hokan-shohsho o misetay kuda-sai.* 保険証書を見せてください。
Will you act as a witness?	*Shohnin ni nat-tay kuremas-ka?* 証人になってくれますか？
I need the details for the insurance.	*Hoken no tame ni shoh-sai ga hits-yoh des.* 保険のために詳細が必要です。
Are you insured?	*Hoken ni hait-tay imas-ka?* 保険に入っていますか？
Could you sign here, please?	*Koko ni sign o shtay kuda-sai.* ここにサインをしてください。

14.4 Theft

I've been robbed.	*Nusu-mare-mashta.* 盗まれました。
My...has been stolen.	*... ga nusu-mare-mashta.* …が盗まれました。

14.5 Missing person

I've lost my child/ grandmother.	*Kodomo/sobo ga maigo ni nari-mashta.* 子供／祖母が迷子になりました。
Could you help me find him/her?	*Sagasu no o tetsudat-tay kuda-sai.* 捜すのを手伝ってください。
Have you seen a small child?	*Chee-sai ko o mi-masen-deshta-ka?* 小さい子を見ませんでしたか？

He's/she's...years old.	*... sai des.* ···歳です。
He's got short blond/red/ brown/black/gray hair.	*Kami ga miji-kai kimpats/a-kai/cha-iro/ kuro-i/hakuhats des.* 髪が短い金髪／赤い／茶色／黒い／白髪です。
She's got long curly/ straight/frizzy hair.	*Kami ga na-gai maki-ge/mas-sugu/ chijirege des.* 髪が長い巻き毛／真っ直ぐ／縮れ毛です。
Her hair is in a ponytail.	*Kanojo wa kami o ponee-tehru ni shtay imas.* 彼女は髪を ポニーテールにしています。
Her hair is in braids.	*Kanojo wa kami o mitsu-ami ni shtay imas.* 彼女は髪を三つ編みにしています。
Her hair is in a bun.	*Kanojo wa kami o tabane-tay imas.* 彼女は髪をたばねています。
He's/she's got blue eyes.	*Me ga ao-i des.* 目が青いです。
He's/she's got brown eyes.	*Me ga cha-iro des.* 目が茶色です。
He's wearing swimming trunks.	*Kai-swee pants o hai-tay imas.* 海水パンツをはいています。
He's wearing hiking boots.	*Tohzan-guts o hai-tay imas.* 登山靴をはいています。
He has glasses.	*Meganay o kaketay imas.* 眼鏡をかけています。
He's tall.	*Oh-kee des.* 大きいです。
He's short.	*Chee-sai des.* 小さいです。
This is a photo of him/her.	*Kare/kanoji no shashin des.* 彼／彼女の写真です。

14.6 The police

運転免許証を見せてください。 Your driving license, please.
スピード違反です。 You were speeding.

ここは駐車禁止です。 You're not allowed to park here.
ライトがついていません。 Your lights aren't working.
罰金は…円です。 That's a...yen fine.
今払いますか? Do you want to pay now?
今払わなければなりません。 You'll have to pay now.

I don't speak Japanese.	*Nihon-go ga hanase-masen.* 日本語が話せません。
I didn't see the sign.	*Ano kohtsoo-hyohshiki ga mie-masen deshta.* あの交通標識が見えませんでした。
I don't understand what it says.	*Ano hyohshiki wa wakari-masen.* あの標識は分かりません。
I was only doing... kilometers an hour.	*Jisoku ...kiro dake de hashit-tay imashta.* 時速…キロだけで走っていました。
I'll have my car checked.	*Kuruma o kensa shte-morai-mas.* 車を検査してもらいます。
I was blinded by oncoming lights.	*Tai-koh-sha no raito ni me ga kurami-mashta.* 対向車のライトに目がくらみました。

At the police station

I want to report a collision.	*Shohtots o todoke ni kimashta.* 衝突を届けに来ました。
I want to report a missing. person.	*Maigo o todoke ni kimashta.* まい子を届けに来ました。
I want to report a rape.	*Gohkan o todoke ni kimashta.* 強姦を届けに来ました。
Could you write a report, please?	*Chohsho o kai-tay kuda-sai.* 調書を書いてください。
Could I have a copy for the insurance?	*Hoken no tame ni utsushi o kuda-sai.* 保険のために写しをください。

どこで起こりましたか？ Where did it happen?

何をなくしましたか？ What's missing?

何が盗まれましたか？ What's been taken?

身分証明書を見せてください。 Could I see some identification?

それは何時でしたか？ What time did it happen?

誰が関係しましたか？ Who was involved?

証人がいますか？ Are there any witnesses?

ここに記入してください。 Fill this out, please.

ここにサインをしてください。 Sign here, please.

通訳が必要ですか？ Do you want an interpreter?

I've lost everything.	*Zembu ushi-nai-mashta.* 全部失いました。
I've lost all my money.	*Okane ga zembu nakunari-mashta.* お金が全部なくなりました。
Could you lend me some money?	*Okane o skoshi kashtay kuda-sai-masen-ka?* お金を少し貸してくださいますか?
I'd like an interpreter.	*Tsooyaku ga hits-yoh des.* 通訳が必要です。
I'm innocent.	*Watashi wa muzai des.* 私は無罪です。
I don't know anything about it.	*Nan-ni mo shiri-masen.* 何も知りません。
I want to speak to someone from the American embassy.	*Amerika ryohjikan no hito to hanashi-tai-n des.* アメリカ領事館の人と話したいんです。
I want to speak to someone from the British consulate.	*Igirisu tai-shikan no hito to hanashi-tai-n des.* イギリス大使館の人と話したいんです。
I want a lawyer who speaks English.	*Aygo ga hanaseru bengoshi ga hitsyoh des.* 英語が話せる弁護士が必要です。

15. English-Japanese Dictionary

The following dictionary is meant to supplement the chapters in this book. Where a word has more than one meaning, notes have been inserted to show how it is used. Some words not in this list can be found elsewhere in the book, e.g., alongside the diagrams of the car, bicycle and camping equipment.

A

above	*ue*	上
abroad	*gai-kok*	外国
abundant	*hohfu na*	豊富な
accident	*jiko*	事故
adapter	*adapu-tah*	アダプター
adder	*mamushi*	マムシ
addition	*kaysan*	計算
address	*joo-sho*	住所
admission	*nyoojoh*	入場
admission price	*nyoojoh-ryoh*	入場料
advice	*choo-kok*	忠告
after	*... no ato de*	…の後で
afternoon	*gogo*	午後
aftershave	*aftah-shayb rohshon*	アフターシェーブローション
again	*moh ichido*	もう一度
against	*... ni tai-shtay*	…に対して
age	*nen-ray*	年齢
AIDS	*Ayz*	エイズ
air conditioning	*e-a-kon*	エアコン
air mattress	*e-a mattores*	エア・マットレス
airplane	*hikohki*	飛行機
airport	*kookoh*	空港
airport hotel	*kookoh no hoteru*	空港のホテル
airport security	*kookoh-keibi/ kookoh-sekyuritee*	空港警備／ 空港セキュリティー
aisle seat	*tsoo-ro gawa no seki*	通路側の席
alarm	*kay-kok*	警告
alarm clock	*mezamashi-dokay*	目覚まし時計
alcohol	*aru-kohru*	アルコール
all the time	*zutto*	ずっと
allergic	*areru-gee*	アレルギー
alone	*hitori de*	一人で
always	*its-mo*	いつも
ambulance	*kyoo-kyoo-sha*	救急車
America	*Amerika*	アメリカ

American	*Amerika-jin*	アメリカ人
amount	*soh-gak*	総額
amusement park	*yoo-en-chi*	遊園地
anesthetize (local)	*kyokusho-maswee o kakeru*	局所麻酔をかける
anchovy	*anchobee*	アンチョビー
angry	*okotta*	おこった
animal	*doh-buts*	動物
anime/game store	*anime/gehm sentah*	アニメ／ゲームセンター
ankle	*kurubushi*	くるぶし
answer	*ko-ta-e/henji*	答え／返事
ant	*ari*	アリ
antibiotics	*kohsay bu-shits*	抗生物質
antifreeze	*fu-toh-eki*	不凍液
antique (adj)	*kodai no*	古代の
antiques	*kobijuts/kottoh-hin*	古美術／骨董品
anus	*kohmon*	肛門
apartment	*a-pahto*	アパート
aperitif	*shokuzen-shu*	食前酒
apologies	*yurushi*	許し
app (application)	*apuri*	アプリ
apple	*ringo*	リンゴ
apple juice	*ringo joos*	リンゴジュース
apple pie	*appuru pai*	アップルパイ
apple sauce	*appuru sohsu*	アップルソース
application	*apuri-kay-shon*	アプリケーション
appointment	*yak-soku*	約束
apricot	*anzu*	アンズ
April	*Shi-gats*	四月
architecture	*ken-chiku*	建築
area	*kankyoh*	環境
area code	*shi-gai kyokuban*	市外局番
arm	*uday*	腕
arrange	*yak-soku suru*	約束する
arrive	*tsuku*	着く
arrow	*ya-jirushi*	矢印
art	*gay-juts*	芸術
artery	*doh-myaku*	動脈
article	*mono*	物
artificial respiration	*jinkoh kokyoo*	人口呼吸
ashtray	*hai-zara*	灰皿
ask	*tazuneru/tou*	尋ねる／問う
ask (for)	*tanomu*	頼む
asparagus	*asparagas*	アスパラガス
aspirin	*aspirin*	アスピリン
assault	*gohkan*	強姦
at @	*atto-mah-ku*	アットマーク
at home	*uchi ni*	家に
at night	*yoru*	夜
at the back	*ushiro ni*	後に
at the front	*ma-e ni*	前に
at the latest	*osokutemo*	遅くても
ATM card	*cash kah-do*	キャッシュカード

August	*Hachi-gats*	八月
automatic	*jidoh-teki*	自動的
autumn	*aki*	秋
avalanche	*nadaray*	雪崩
awake	*okita*	起きた
awning	*hiyokay*	日よけ

B

baby	*aka-chan*	赤ちゃん
baby sitter	*baybee-shittah*	ベビーシッター
back	*senaka*	背中
backpack	*ryukku-sakku*	リュックサック
bacon	*behkon*	ベーコン
bad	*waru-i*	悪い
bad (terrible)	*hidoi/tai-hen*	ひどい／大変
bag	*kaban*	カバン
baggage claim	*te-nimots uke-tori-jo*	手荷物受取所
baggage claim check	*te-nimots hiki-kae-ken*	手荷物引換券
baker	*pan-ya*	パン屋
balcony	*barukonee*	バルコニー
ball	*bohru/tama*	ボール／球
ballet	*baray*	バレエ
ballpoint pen	*bohru-pen*	ボールペン
banana	*banana*	バナナ
bandage	*hoh-tai*	包帯
Bandaids	*Bansohkoh*	バンソウコウ
bangs	*ma-e-gami*	前髪
bank	*gin-koh*	銀行
bank (river)	*kishi*	岸
bar (café)	*bah/boh*	バー／棒
bar	*bah*	バー
barbecue	*bahbekyoo*	バーベキュー
basketball (to play)	*basketto-bohru*	バスケットボール
bath	*furo/bas*	風呂／バス
bath towel	*bas-taoru*	バスタオル
bathing cap	*kai-swee boh*	海水帽
bathing suit	*mizu-gi*	水着
bathroom	*furo-ba/bas-room*	風呂場／バスルーム
battery	*betteree/denchi*	バッテリー／電池
beach	*hama/beechi*	浜／ビーチ
beans	*mamay*	豆
beautiful	*subara-shee/kabi na*	すばらしい／華美な
beautiful	*utsuku-shee/kiray na*	美しい／きれいな
beauty parlor	*biyoh-in*	美容院
bed	*beddo/shin-dai*	ベッド／寝台
bee	*mitsu-bachi*	ミツバチ
beef	*gyoo-niku*	牛肉
beer	*beeru*	ビール
begin	*haji-maru*	始まる
beginner	*sho-shin-sha*	初心者
behind	*ushiro*	後
belt	*beruto*	ベルト

berth	*shin-dai*	寝台
better (to get)	*genki ni naru/kai-fuku suru*	元気になる／快復する
bicarbonate of soda	*jootan-san sohda*	重炭酸ソーダ
bicycle	*jitensha*	自転車
bicycle pump	*kooki-iray*	空気入れ
bicycle shop (to fix)	*jitensha-ya*	自転車屋
bikini	*bikini*	ビキニ
bill	*kanjoh*	勘定
billiards (to play)	*tama-tski o suru*	玉突きをする
birthday	*tanjoh-bi*	誕生日
biscuit	*bisketto/kukkee*	ビスケット／クッキー
bite	*kamu*	かむ
bitter	*ni-gai*	苦い
black	*kuro-i*	黒い
bland (taste)	*aji no nai*	味のない
blanket	*mohf*	毛布
bleach	*hyoh-hak suru/dasshok suru*	漂白する／脱色する
blister	*mizu-buku-ray*	水膨れ
blond	*kimpats*	金髪
blood	*kets-eki*	血液
blood pressure	*kets-ats*	血圧
bloody nose	*hana-ji*	鼻血
blouse	*burausu*	ブラウス
blow dry	*(kami o) kawakas*	(髪を)乾かす
blue	*a-oi*	青い
blunt	*nibui*	鈍い
boarding pass	*toh-joe-ken*	搭乗券
boat	*bohto*	ボート
body	*karada*	体
boiled	*yudeta*	茹でた
boiled ham	*hamu*	ハム
bonbon	*bonbon*	ボンボン
bone	*honay*	骨
bonnet	*bon-netto*	ボンネット
book	*hon*	本
booked (theater ticket)	*yoyaku shta/zumi no*	予約した／済みの
booking office (theater ticket)	*puray-gaido/kippu uri-ba*	プレイガイド／切符売り場
bookshop	*hon-ya*	本屋
border	*kok-kyoh*	国境
bored (to be)	*akita*	飽きた
boring	*omoshi-roku-nai/ tsumara-nai*	面白くない／つまらない
born	*umareta*	生まれた
borrow (from)	*(kara) kariru*	(から)借りる
botanical gardens	*shokubutsu-en*	植物園
both	*ryoh-hoh*	両方
bottle	*bin*	びん
bottle (baby's)	*honyoo-bin*	哺乳びん
bottle-warmer	*honyoo-bin ho-on-ki*	哺乳びん保温器
bowling	*bohring o suru*	ボーリングをする
box	*hako*	箱
box office	*puray-gaido/chiketto uri-ba*	プレイガイド/チケット売り場

box (in theater)	*bokks-seki-de*	ボックス席で
boy	*otoko-no-ko*	男の子
bra	*burajah*	ブラジャー
bracelet	*uday-wa/bures-retto*	腕輪／ブレスレット
braised	*nikonda*	煮込んだ
brake	*brayki*	ブレーキ
brake oil	*brayki-oiru*	ブレーキオイル
bread	*pan*	パン
break	*oru*	折る
breakfast	*asa-gohan*	朝ご飯
breast	*munay*	胸
breast milk	*bonyoo*	母乳
bridge	*hashi*	橋
briefs	*pants/pantee*	パンツ／パンティー
bring	*mot-tay kuru*	持ってくる
brochure	*panf-retto*	パンフレット
broken	*yabureta/kowareta*	破れた／こわれた
brother (older, others')	*o-nee-san*	お兄さん
brother (older, own)	*ani*	兄
brother (younger, others')	*o-tohto-san*	弟さん
brother (younger, own)	*o-tohto*	弟
brown	*cha-iro*	茶色
browser	*burauza*	ブラウザ
bruise	*aza ga dekiru*	あざができる
brush	*burashi*	ブラシ
brussel sprouts	*me-kyabets*	芽キャベツ
bucket	*bakets*	バケツ
bugs	*gai-choo/bai-kin*	害虫／ばい菌
building	*tate-mono*	建物
built-in	*toh-sai*	搭載
bun	*kashi-pan*	菓子パン
buoy	*bui*	ブイ
burglary	*oshikomi*	押し込み
burn	*yakedo*	火傷
burn (verb)	*yakeru*	焼ける
burnt	*yai-ta*	焼いた
bus	*bas*	バス
bus station	*bas no hat-chaku-jo*	バスの発着所
bus stop	*bas-tay*	バス停
business class	*bijinesu-kuras*	ビジネスクラス
business trip	*shut-choh*	出張
busy (schedule)	*isogashee*	忙しい
busy (traffic)	*konzats*	混雑
butane gas	*butan-gas*	ブタン・ガス
butcher	*niku-ya*	肉屋
butter	*batah*	バター
button	*botan*	ボタン
buy	*ka-u*	買う
by airmail	*kohkoobin de*	航空便で
by phone	*denwa de*	電話で

156

c

cabbage	*kyabets*	キャベツ
cabin	*sen-shits*	船室
cake	*kehki*	ケーキ
cake shop	*kehki-ya/okashi-ya*	ケーキ屋／お菓子屋
call	*yobi-dashi*	呼び出し
call (phone)	*denwa o suru*	電話をする
called (name)	*... to yoo/... to eemas*	…と言う／…と言います
camera	*kamera*	カメラ
camera shake correction (feature)	*tebure hosei kinoh*	手ぶれ補正機能
camp (verb)	*kyampu suru*	キャンプする
camp shop	*kyampu-jo no bai-ten*	キャンプ場の売店
camp site	*kyampu-jo*	キャンプ場
camper	*kyamping-kah*	キャンピングカー
campfire	*kyampu-fai-yah*	キャンプファイヤー
camping guide	*kyampu gaido*	キャンプガイド
camping permit	*kyampu-jo shiyoh kyoka-sho*	キャンプ場使用 許可書
cancel	*tori-kes*	取り消す
candle	*rohsok*	ローソク
candy	*okashi/oyats*	お菓子／おやつ
canoe	*ka-noo*	カヌー
car	*kuruma/jidoh-sha*	車／自動車
car deck	*jidoh-sha-yoh no kampan*	自動車用の甲板
car documents	*kuruma no shohmay-sho*	車の証明書
car seat (child's)	*bebee sheeto*	ベビーシート
car trouble	*kuruma no koshoh*	車の故障
caravan	*kyaraban*	キャラバン
cardigan	*kahdigan*	カーディガン
careful	*choo-i-bu-kai*	注意深い
carrot	*ninjin*	にんじん
carriage	*uba-guruma/baybee-kah*	乳母車／ベビーカー
cartridge	*kahtorigge*	カートリッジ
cascade	*taki*	滝
cash desk	*shi-harai-jo*	支払い所
casino	*kajino*	カジノ
cassette	*kasetto-tehpu*	カセット・テープ
castle	*shiro*	城
cat	*neko*	猫
catalogue	*katarog*	カタログ
cathedral	*dai-say-doh*	大聖堂
cauliflower	*kari-fura-wah*	カリフラワー
cave	*hora-ana*	ほら穴
CD	*shee-dee*	シーディー
celebrate	*iwau*	祝う
cell phone	*kay-tai denwa/kay-tai*	携帯電話/携帯
cemetery	*bochi*	墓地
center	*... no naka no*	…の中の
center (city)	*choo-shin-chi*	中心地
centimeter	*senchi (meh-toru)*	センチ（メートル）
central heating	*sentoraru-hee-ting*	セントラル・ヒーティング
chair	*isu*	椅子

chambermaid	kyakushits-gakari	客室係
champagne	shampen	シャンペン
change	kaeru	変える
change (money)	ryoh-ga-e	両替
change (money) (verb)	ryoh-ga-e suru	両替する
change (trains)	nori-ka-eru	乗り換える
change the baby's diaper	omuts o tori-ka-eru	おむつを取り替える
change the oil	oiru o kohkan suru	オイルを交換する
charger	joo-den-ki	充電器
charter flight	chahtah-bin	チャーター便
chat	oshaberi (suru)	おしゃべり（する）
check	chekk (suru)	チェック（する）
check	kogit-tay	小切手
checked luggage	te-nimots ichi-ji azukari-jo	手荷物一時預かり所
check-in	chekku-in	チェックイン
cheers	kam-pai	乾杯
cheese	cheez	チーズ
chef	kokku-san	コックさん
cherries	cheree/sakurambo	チェリー／サクランボ
chess (to play)	chesu o suru	チェスをする
chewing gum	chooing-gam	チューインガム
chicken	niwatori	ニワトリ
child (others')	okosan	お子さん
child (own)	kodomo	子供
child's seat	kodomo-yoh isu	子供用いす
chilled	hieta	冷えた
chin	ago	あご
chocolate	choko-rayto	チョコレート
choose	sentaku suru/erabu	選択する／選ぶ
chop (with breadcrumbs)	katsurets	カツレツ
chop (meat)	hiki-niku	挽き肉
church	kyoh-kai	教会
church service	ray-hai	礼拝
cigar	hamaki	葉巻
cigar shop	tabako-ya	たばこ屋
cigarette	tabako	たばこ
circle	en	円
circus	sahkas	サーカス
city	shi	市
clean	saykets na	清潔な
clean (verb)	sohji suru	掃除する
clear	hak-kiri shta	はっきりした
clearance (sale)	sehru	セール
clock	to-kay	時計
closed	shmat-tay-iru	閉まっている
closed off (road)	tsoo-koh domay	通行止め
clothes	ifu-ku	衣服
clothes hanger	han-gah	ハンガー
clothes pin	sentaku-basami	洗濯ばさみ
clothing	i-rui	衣類
cloud computing	kuraudo	クラウド
coat	kohto	コート
cockroach	gokiburi/abura-mushi	ゴキブリ／アブラムシ

cocoa	*koko-a*	ココア
cod	*tara*	タラ
coffee	*koh-hee*	コーヒー
coffee filter	*koh-hee firutah*	コーヒー・フィルター
cognac	*konyakku*	コニャック
cold (flu)	*kazay*	風邪
cold (not hot)	*samu-i*	寒い
collarbone	*sakots*	鎖骨
colleague	*doh-ryoh*	同僚
collision	*shoh-tots*	衝突
cologne	*keshoh-swee*	化粧水
color	*iro*	色
color pencils	*iro-empits*	色鉛筆
color television	*karah-terebi*	カラーテレビ
coloring book	*nuri-e no hon*	ぬり絵の本
comb	*kushi*	くし
come	*kuru*	来る
come back	*modot-tay kuru*	戻って来る
compartment	*kompahtomento*	コンパートメント
complaint	*kujoh*	苦情
complaint (illness)	*itami*	痛み
completely	*mattaku*	全く
compliment	*sanji*	賛辞
compulsory	*gimu*	義務
computer	*paso-kon*	パソコン
concert (classical)	*konsahto*	コンサート
concert hall	*konsahto-hohru*	コンサートホール
concussion	*noh-shintoh*	脳しんとう
condensed milk	*kureem*	クリーム
condom	*kondohm*	コンドーム
congratulate	*iwa-u*	祝う
connection	*setsu-zoku*	接続
constipation	*bempi*	便秘
consulate	*ryohji-kan*	領事館
consultation (house call by doctor)	*ohshin*	往診
contact lens	*kontakuto-renzu*	コンタクトレンズ
contagious	*densensay no*	伝染性の
contraceptive	*hinin no*	避妊の
contraceptive pill	*hinin-yak/piru*	避妊薬／ピル
convenience store	*kom-bini*	コンビニ
cook	*kokku*	コック
cook (verb)	*ryohri suru*	料理する
copper	*doh*	銅
copy	*kopee*	コピー
corkscrew	*koruk-nuki*	コルク抜き
corn flour	*kohn-stahchi*	コーンスターチ
corner	*sumi/kado*	隅／角
correct	*tada-shee*	正しい
correspond	*bun-tsoo suru*	文通する
corridor	*rohka*	廊くだ
cosplay shop	*cosplay shoppu*	コスプレショップ
costume	*i-show*	衣装

cot	*bebee-beddo*	ベビーベッド
cotton	*momen*	木綿
cotton antiseptic	*dasshi-men/wata*	脱脂綿／綿
cough	*seki*	咳
cough (verb)	*seki-komu*	咳込む
cough syrup	*seki-domay shiroppu*	咳止めシロップ
counter	*uke-tskay*	受付け
country (nation)	*kuni*	国
country (rural area)	*inaka*	田舎
country code	*kuni ban-go*	国番号
course (of treatment)	*chi-ryoh*	治療
cousin	*itoko*	いとこ
crab	*kani*	蟹
cream	*kureem*	クリーム
cream (fresh)	*nama-kureemu*	生クリーム
credit card	*kurejitto-kahdo*	クレジット・カード
croissant	*kuro-wasson*	クロワッサン
cross the road	*ohdan suru*	横断する
cross-country run	*kuros-kantoree-skee-yoh no kohs*	クロスカントリースキー用のコース
cross-country skiing	*kuros-kantoree-skee*	クロスカントリー スキー
cross-country skis	*kuros-kantoree-yoh-skee*	クロスカントリー用 スキー
cry	*naku*	泣く
cubic meter	*rippoh meh-toru*	立方メートル
cucumber	*kyoori*	キュウリ
cuddly toy	*nui-gurumi*	ぬいぐるみ
cuff links	*kafs-botan*	カフス・ボタン
cup	*chawan*	茶わん
curly	*maki-ge no*	巻き毛の
current	*nagaray/denryoo*	流れ／電流
cursor	*cah-soru*	カーソル
cushion	*kusshon*	クッション
customary	*futsoo/its-mo*	普通／いつも
customs	*zaykan*	税関
cut	*kiru*	切る
cutlery	*naif to fohk to spoon*	ナイフとフォークとスプーン
cybercafe	*intah-netto kafe*	インターネットカフェ
cycling	*sai-ku-ring*	サイクリング

D

dairy products	*nyoo-say-hin*	乳製品
damage	*son-gai*	損害
dance	*odoru*	踊る
dandruff	*fu-kay*	ふけ
danger	*kiken*	危険
dangerous	*kiken na*	危険な
dark	*ku-rai*	暗い
date	*dayto*	デート
daughter (others')	*musu-may-san*	娘さん
daughter (own)	*musu-may*	娘
day	*hi*	日
day (the whole)	*maru ichi-nichi*	まる一日
day before yesterday	*ototoi*	一昨日

day-trip hot spring	*higa-eri-onsen*	日帰り温泉
dead	*nakunatta*	亡くなった
dead zone	*deddo zohn*	デッドゾーン
decaffeinated	*kafayn-nashi/kafayn-free*	カフェインなし／カフェインフリー
December	*Joo-ni-gats*	十二月
deck chair	*beechi-cheyah*	ビーチ・チェアー
declare (customs)	*shin-koku suru*	申告する
deep	*fu-kai*	深い
deep sea diving	*skin-dai-bing*	スキンダイビング
deep freeze	*raytoh-ko*	冷凍庫
degrees	*do*	度
delay	*tay-tai/chi-en*	停滞／遅延
delicious	*o-ishee*	おいしい
dentist	*ha-isha*	歯医者
dentures	*ireba*	入れ歯
deodorant	*deodoranto*	デオドラント
department	*bu*	部
department store	*depahto*	デパート
departure	*shuppats*	出発
departure time	*shuppats jikan*	出発時間
deposit	*te-tsuke-kin/atama-kin*	手付け金／頭金
deposit (for safekeeping)	*hokan*	保管
dessert	*dezahto*	デザート
destination	*yuki-saki*	行き先
destination (terminal)	*shooten*	終点
develop (photo)	*genzoh suru*	現像する
developer (of software)	*(sofuto-wea no) kai-hats-sha*	（ソフトウェアの）開発者
diabetic	*toh-nyoh-byoh kanja*	糖尿病患者
dial	*dai-yaru*	ダイヤル
diamond	*dai-a-mondo*	ダイヤモンド
diaper	*o-shimay*	おしめ
diarrhea	*geri*	下痢
dictionary	*jiten*	辞典
diesel/diesel oil	*deezeru*	ディーゼル
diet	*dai-etto*	ダイエット
difficulty	*kon-nan*	困難
digital camera	*deji-kame*	デジカメ
digital single-lens reflex camera	*deji-taru ichi-gun-refu*	デジタル一眼レフ
dining room	*shoku-doh*	食堂
dining/buffet car	*shokudoh-sha/buffay-kah*	食堂車／ビュッフェカー
dinner	*dinah*	ディナー
dinner (to have)	*dinah o taberu*	ディナーを食べる
direction	*hohkoh*	方向
directly	*choku-sets ni*	直接に
dirty	*kita-nai/yogoreta*	きたない／汚れた
disabled	*shoh-gai-sha*	障害者
disco	*disko*	ディスコ
discount	*wari-biki*	割引
dish	*hito-sara/ip-pin*	一皿／一品
dish of the day	*kyoh no ryohri*	今日の料理
disinfectant	*shohdoku-zai*	消毒剤

distance	*kyori*	距離
distilled water	*joh-ryoo-swee*	蒸留水
disturb	*jama suru*	じゃまする
disturbance	*boh-gai*	妨害
dive	*moguru*	潜る
diving	*dai-bing*	ダイビング
diving board	*tobikomi-dai*	飛び込み台
diving gear	*dai-bing-setto*	ダイビング・セット
divorced	*rikon shta*	離婚した
Do-it-yourself store	*hohm-sentah*	ホームセンター
dizzy	*me-mai*	めまい
do	*suru*	する
doctor	*isha*	医者
dog	*inu*	犬
doll	*ningyoh*	人形
domestic	*koku-nai*	国内
done (cooked)	*chohri shta*	調理した
door	*to/doa*	戸／ドア
dot	*dotto*	ドット
double	*daburu*	ダブル
down	*shta*	下
download	*down-roh-do*	ダウンロード
draft (air)	*skima-kazay*	すき間風
dream (verb)	*(... o) yumay ni miru*	(…を) 夢に見る
dress	*dores*	ドレス
dressing gown	*heya-gi*	部屋着
drink (medicine)	*kusuri o nomu*	薬を飲む
drink (verb)	*nomu*	飲む
drinking water	*inryoh-swee*	飲料水
drive	*unten suru*	運転する
driver	*unten-shu*	運転手
driver's licence	*unten menkyo-shoh*	運転免許証
druggist	*yak-kyoku*	薬局
dry	*kawa-ita*	かわいた
dry (verb)	*hosu*	干す
dry clean	*drai-kree-ningu*	ドライクリーニング
dry cleaners	*sentaku-ya/kree-ningu-ten*	洗濯屋／クリーニング店
during	*... choo*	…中
during (in the middle of)	*... no ai-da ni*	…の間に
during the day	*hiruma*	昼間

E

ear	*mimi*	耳
ear, nose and throat specialist	*jibi-inkoh-ka*	耳鼻・咽喉科
earache	*mimi no itami*	耳の痛み
earbud	*e-ya-hon*	イヤホン
eardrops	*ten-ji-yaku*	点耳薬
early	*haya-i*	早い
earrings	*e-ya-ring*	イヤリング
earth	*to-chi*	土地
earthenware	*toh-ki*	陶器
east	*higashi*	東

easy (simple)	*kantan na/yoh-i na*	簡単な／容易な
easy (to use)	*benri na*	便利な
eat	*taberu*	食べる
e-book	*denshi-shoseki/ee-bukku*	電子書籍／Eブック
e-booking/reservations	*ee-buk-kingu*	E-ブッキング
eczema	*shisshin*	湿疹
eel	*unagi*	ウナギ
egg	*tamago*	卵
eggplant	*nasu*	ナス
electric	*denki (no)*	電気（の）
electric bicycle	*dendoh jiten-sha*	電動自転車
electric car	*denki jidoh-sha*	電気自動車
electricity	*denki*	電気
electronics shop	*denki-ya*	電気屋
elevator	*ere-behtah*	エレベーター
email	*ee-may-ru*	Eメール
embassy	*tai-shikan*	大使館
emergency brake	*kinkyoo brayki*	緊急ブレーキ
emergency exit	*hijoh-guchi*	非常口
emergency phone	*hijoh denwa*	非常電話
emperor	*ten-noh*	天皇
empty	*kara no*	空の
engaged (on the phone)	*hanashi-choo*	話し中
engaged (to be married)	*kon-yak-shta*	婚約した
English (language)	*Ay-go*	英語
enjoy	*tano-shimu*	楽しむ
envelope	*footoh*	封筒
e-reader	*denji-shoseki reader*	電子書籍リーダー
escort	*kompanion*	コンパニオン
e-ticket	*ee-chiketto*	Eチケット
ethnology	*minzoku-gaku*	民族学
evening	*yoo-gata*	夕方
evening wear	*dinah soots (men)/ebu-ningu dores (women)*	ディナースーツ／イブニングドレス
event	*jiken/dekigoto*	事件／できごと
everything	*zembu*	全部
everywhere	*doko ni-mo*	どこにも
examine	*saguru*	探る
excavation	*hakkuts*	発掘
excellent	*sugureta*	優れた
exchange	*kohkan suru*	交換する
exchange office	*kawase-ryoh-gae-jo*	為替両替所
exchange rate	*kawase-rayto*	為替レート
excursion	*yooran*	遊覧
exhibition	*tenran-kai*	展覧会
exit	*deguchi*	出口
expenses	*hiyoh/kayhi*	費用／経費
expensive	*ta-kai*	高い
explain	*setsumay suru*	説明する
express	*kyookoh densha*	急行電車
extension	*nai-sen bangoh*	内線番号
external	*soto*	外
eye	*me*	目

eye drops	me-gusuri	目薬
eye shadow	ai-shadoh	アイシャドー
eye specialist	ganka-i/me-isha	眼科医／目医者
eyeliner	ai-rainah	アイライナー

F

face	kao	顔
facial-recognition camera	kao nin-shiki kamera	顔認識カメラ
factory	koh-joh	工場
fall (verb)	korobu	転ぶ
family	kazoku	家族
famous	yoo-may na	有名な
far away	tohku	遠く
farm	noh-ka	農家
farmer	noh-min	農民
fashion	fashon	ファッション
fast	ha-yai	速い
father (others')	o-toh-sama	お父さま
father (own)	chichi/o-toh-san	父／お父さん
fault	ayamari	誤り
fax (verb)	fakks o okuru	ファックスを送る
February	Ni-gats	二月
feel	kanjiru	感じる
feel like	konomu	好む
fence	kaki-ne	垣根
ferry	watasi-bunay/feree-bohto	渡し船／フェリーボート
fever	nets	熱
fill	tsumeru	詰める
fill out	kaki-komu	書き込む
filling	tsumemono	詰め物
film (cinema)	ayga	映画
film (photo)	firumu	フィルム
filter	firutah	フィルター
filter cigarette	firutah-tski tabako	フィルター付きタバコ
find	mits-keru	見つける
fine (money)	bakkin	罰金
finger	yubi	指
fire	hi	火
fire (on)	kaji	火事
fire dept.	shoh-boh	消防
fire escape	hijoh kai-dan	非常階段
fire extinguisher	shoh-ka-ki	消火器
first (in line)	sai-sho ni	最初に
first (number one)	dai-ichi/ichiban	第一／一番
first aid	ohkyoo te-atay	応急手当て
first class	it-toh	一等
fish	sakana	魚
fish (verb)	tsuri o suru	釣をする
fishing rod	tsuri-zao	釣竿
fitness club	fitnes-sentah	フィットネスセンター
fitness training	fitnes	フィットネス
fitting room	shichaku-shits	試着室

fix (puncture)	*panku shta tai-ya o na-osu*	パンクしたタイヤを 直す
flag	*hata*	旗
flash	*furas-shu*	フラッシュ
flea market	*nomi-no-ichi*	蚤の市
flight	*hikoh*	飛行
flight number	*bin-may*	便名
flood	*ohmizu*	大水
floor	*kai*	階
flour	*kona*	粉
flu	*infruenza*	インフルエンザ
fly (insect)	*ha-e*	ハエ
fly (verb)	*tobu*	飛ぶ
fog	*kiri*	霧
foggy (to be)	*kiri ga kakaru*	霧がかかる
follow	*shita-ga-u*	従う
food (items)	*shokuhin*	食品
food (stuffs)	*shoku-ryoh*	食料
food poisoning	*shoku-choodoku*	食中毒
foot	*ashi*	足
forbidden	*kinshi*	禁止
forehead	*hi-tai*	額
foreign	*gai-koku no*	外国の
forest bathing	*shin-rin-yoku*	森林浴
forget	*wasureru*	忘れる
fork	*fohku*	フォーク
form	*yohshi*	用紙
forward (a letter)	*ten-soh suru*	転送する
fountain	*fun-swee*	噴水
frame	*gaku-buchi*	額縁
free (no charge)	*muryoh*	無料
free (unoccupied)	*ai-tay iru*	空いている
free time	*hima*	暇
freeze	*kohru*	凍る
French bread	*Furansu-pan*	フランスパン
french fries	*fraido-poteto*	フライドポテト
fresh	*shinsen na*	新鮮な
Friday	*Kin-yohbi*	金曜日
fried	*yai-ta*	焼いた
fried egg	*medama-yaki*	目玉焼き
friend	*tomo-dachi*	友達
friendly	*kokoro-kara no/shinsetu na*	心からの／親切な
frightened	*osoreru*	恐れる
fruit	*froots/kudamono*	フルーツ／果物
fruit juice	*joosu*	ジュース
frying pan	*furai-pan*	フライパン
full (tank)	*mantan*	満タン
fun	*tano-shee*	楽しい

G

gallery	*garoh*	画廊
game	*gehm*	ゲーム
garage (car repair)	*shoori-ya*	修理屋

garbage bag	gomi-bukuro	ごみ袋
garden	niwa	庭
gas	gasorin	ガソリン
gas station	gasorin stando	ガソリンスタンド
gear	gee-a	ギア
geek	otaku	オタク
gel (hair)	jeru/sei-hats-ryoh	ジェル／整髪料
get married	kekkon suru	結婚する
get off	gesha suru/oriru	下車する／降りる
gift	okuri-mono/gift	贈り物／ギフト
gilt	kin-mekki	金メッキ
ginger	shoh-ga	ショウガ
girl	on'na-no-ko	女の子
girlfriend	gahru-frendo/kanojo	ガールフレンド／彼女
giro check	kogit-tay	小切手
given name	nama-e	名前
glass	garas	ガラス
glass (drinking)	guras/koppu	グラス／コップ
glasses	me-ganay	眼鏡
glasses (sun-)	san-guras	サングラス
glide	gu-raidah ni noru	グライダーに乗る
glove	te-bukuro	手袋
glue	nori	のり
gnat (mosquito)	ka	蚊
go	iku	行く
go back	modoru	戻る
go out	gai-shuts suru	外出する
gold	kin	金
golf course	gorufu-jo	ゴルフ場
good afternoon/day	kon-nichi-wa	こんにちは
good evening	kom-ban-wa	こんばんは
good morning	ohayoh gozai-mas	おはようございます
good night	oyasumi-na-sai	おやすみなさい
good bye	sayoh-nara	さようなら
GPS	nabi/kah-nabi	ナビ／カーナビ
grade crossing	fumi-kiri	踏切
gram	gram	グラム
grandchild	mago	孫
grandfather (others')	o-jee-san	おじいさん
grandfather (own)	sofu	祖父
grandmother (others')	obahsan	お婆さん
grandmother (own)	sobo	祖母
grape juice	grayp joosu	グレープ・ジュース
grapefruit	graypu-furoots	グレープフルーツ
grapes	budoh	ブドウ
grave	haka	墓
gray	hai-iro no/nezumi-iro no	灰色の／ねずみ色の
gray (hair)	haku-hats/shiraga	白髪
greasy	abura no oh-ee/aburap-poi	脂の多い／脂っぽい
Great Britain/U.K.	Igirisu	イギリス
green	midori no	緑の
green car	green kah/e-ko kah	グリーンカー／エコカー

greet	*ai-sats suru*	挨拶する
grill	*amiyaki o suru/guriru suru*	網焼きをする／グリルする
grilled	*rohst shta*	ローストした
grocer	*shokuryoh-hin-ten*	食料品店
ground	*tochi*	土地
group	*guroop*	グループ
guest house	*minshuku/penshon*	民宿／ペンション
guide (book)	*annai-sho*	案内書
guide (person)	*gai-do*	ガイド
guided tour	*gai-do tsuki tsu-ah*	ガイド付きツアー
gynecologist	*san-fujin-ka*	産婦人科

H

hacker	*hakkah*	ハッカー
hair	*kami*	髪
hairbrush	*hea-burashi*	ヘアブラシ
hairdresser	*toko-ya/biyoh-in*	床屋／美容院
hairpins	*hea-pin*	ヘアピン
hairspray	*hea-spray*	ヘア・スプレー
half	*hambun*	半分
half full	*... o hambun*	…を半分
hammer	*kana-zuchi*	かなづち
hand	*te*	手
hand brake	*hando-burayki*	ハンド・ブレーキ
handbag	*hando-bag-gu*	ハンドバッグ
handkerchief	*hankachi*	ハンカチ
handmade	*te-zukuri*	手作り
happy	*ure-shee*	うれしい
harbor	*minato*	港
hard	*ka-tai*	堅い
hash mark	*hash mah-ku/sharp*	ハッシュマーク／シャープ
hash tag	*hash-tagu*	ハッシュタグ
hat	*bohshi*	帽子
hay fever	*kafun-shoh*	花粉症
head	*atama*	頭
headache	*zutsoo*	頭痛
health	*kenkoh*	健康
health food shop	*shizen shoku-hin-ten*	自然食品店
hear	*kiku*	聞く
hearing aid	*hochoh-ki*	補聴器
heart	*shinzoh*	心臓
heart patient	*shinzoh-byoh kanja*	心臓病患者
heat	*atsusa*	熱さ
heater	*heetah*	ヒーター
heavy	*omo-i*	重い
heel	*kakato*	かかと
hello	*kon-nichi-wa*	こんにちは
helmet	*herumetto*	ヘルメット
help	*tasukay*	助け
help	*tas-keru/tetsu-dau*	助ける／手伝う
helping (of food)	*ichi-nin-mai*	一人前
herbal tea	*hahbu-tee*	ハーブティー

herbs (seasonings)	*chohmi-ryoh*	調味料
here	*koko*	ここ
herring	*nishin*	ニシン
high	*ta-kai*	高い
high-definition digital camera	*koh-gashits deji-kame*	高画質デジカメ
high tide	*manchoh*	満潮
high chair	*kodomo-yoh no isu*	子供用の椅子
highway	*kohsoku-dohro*	高速道路
hiking	*hai-king*	ハイキング
hiking boots	*to-zan-guts*	登山靴
hip	*koshi*	腰
hire	*chin-tai suru/kariru*	賃貸する／借りる
hitchhike	*hit-chi-hai-ku o suru*	ヒッチハイクをする
hobby	*shumi*	趣味
hold-up	*gohtoh*	強盗
holiday	*kyooka/yasumi*	休暇／休み
holiday (festival)	*sai-jits*	祭日
holiday (public)	*kyoo-jits*	休日
holiday park	*kyoo-ka mura*	休暇村
holiday rental	*bessoh*	別荘
homesickness	*hohm-shikku*	ホームシック
honest	*shoh-jiki na*	正直な
honey	*hachi-mits*	蜂蜜
horizontal	*swee-hay no*	水平の
horrible	*tai-hen*	大変
horse	*uma*	馬
hospital	*byoh-in*	病院
hospitality	*mote-nashi/set-tai*	もてなし／接待
hot	*atsu-i*	熱い／暑い
hot (bitter, sharp)	*ka-rai*	辛い
hot chocolate	*hotto-choko-rayto*	ホットチョコレート
hotspot	*hotto spotto*	ホットスポット
hot spring	*onsen*	温泉
hotel	*hoteru*	ホテル
hot-water bottle	*yoo-tampo*	湯たんぽ
hour	*jikan*	時間
house	*ie/uchi*	家／うち
household items	*nichi-yoh-hin*	日用品
houses of parliament	*kok-kai giji-doh*	国会議事堂
housewife	*shufu*	主婦
how far	*dono gurai (toh-i)*	どのくらい（遠い）
how long	*dono gurai (na-gai)*	どのくらい（長い）
how much	*ikura*	いくら
how	*doh*	どう
hungry (to be)	*koofuku da*	空腹だ
hurry	*kyoosoku*	急速
husband (others')	*goshujin*	ご主人
husband (own)	*otto/shujin*	夫／主人
hut	*koya*	小屋
hybrid car	*hai-brid kah*	ハイブリットカー

I

ice cubes	*kohri*	氷
ice skate	*skehto o suru*	スケートをする
ice cream	*ais-kreem*	アイスクリーム
idea	*kan-ga-e*	考え
identification (card)	*mibun showmay-sho*	身分証明書
identify	*mibun o showmay suru*	身分を証明する
ignition key	*shidoh kee*	始動キー
ill	*byoh-ki no*	病気の
illness	*byoh-ki*	病気
imagine	*sohzoh suru*	想像する
immediately	*sugu-ni*	すぐに
import duty	*yunyoo-zay*	輸入税
impossible	*muri na/fukanoh na*	無理な／不可能な
in	*....no naka-ni*	…の中に
in the evening	*yoogata*	夕方
in the morning	*gozen*	午前
included	*.... o fukumete/fukumeta*	…を含めて／含めた
indicate	*shi-mes*	示す
indicator	*hohkoh-shijiki*	方向指示器
inexpensive	*yasu-i*	安い
infection (viral, bacterial)	*densen (beerus/ bakuteria no)*	伝染（ウイルス／ バクテリアの）
inflammation	*enshoh*	炎症
information	*joh-hoh*	情報
information (guide)	*an-nai*	案内
information (material)	*shiryoh*	資料
information office	*an-nai-sho*	案内所
injection	*choosha*	注射
injured	*fu-shoh shta*	負傷した
innocent	*mu-zai no/muku na*	無罪の／無垢な
insect	*konchoo*	こん虫
insect bite	*mushi-sasaray*	虫さされ
insect repellent	*mushi-yokay kreem*	虫除けクリーム
inside	*naka ni/uchi ni*	中に／内に
insole	*kuts no naka-jiki*	靴の中敷
instructions	*shiyoh-hoh*	使用法
insurance	*hoken*	保険
intermission	*kyookay*	休憩
international	*koku-sai no*	国際の
Internet	*Intah-netto*	インターネット
Internet lounge	*Intah-netto raunji*	インターネットラウンジ
interpreter	*tsooyaku-sha*	通訳者
intersection	*kohsaten*	交差点
introduce (oneself)	*shoh-kai suru*	紹介する
invite	*shoh-tai suru*	招待する
Ireland	*Ai-ru-rando*	アイルランド
iron (clothes)	*ai-ron*	アイロン
iron (metal)	*tets*	鉄
iron (verb)	*ai-ron o kakeru*	アイロンをかける
ironing board	*ai-ron-dai*	アイロン台
island	*shima*	島
itch	*kayui*	かゆい

J

jack	*jakki*	ジャッキ
jacket	*jaketto*	ジャケット
jam	*jamu*	ジャム
January	*Ichi-gats*	一月
Japan Rail Pass	*JR pas*	JRパス
Japanese-style bar	*izakaya*	居酒屋
jaw	*ago*	顎
jellyfish	*kuragay*	クラゲ
jeweler	*kikinzoku-ten/hohseki-ten*	貴金属店／宝石店
jewelry	*soh-shin-gu/hohseki*	装身具／宝石
jog	*joggingu*	ジョギング
joke	*joh-dan*	冗談
juice	*joosu*	ジュース
July	*Shich-gats*	七月
June	*Roku-gats*	六月

K

key	*kee/kagi*	キー／鍵
key (on keyboard)	*key*	キー
keyboard	*key-boad*	キーボード
kilo	*kiro(gram)*	キロ（グラム）
kilometer	*kiro(meh-toru)*	キロ（メートル）
kiss	*kisu*	キス
kiss (verb)	*kisu suru*	キスする
kitchen	*dai-dokoro*	台所
knee	*hiza*	膝
knee socks	*nee-sokkus/hai-sokkus*	ニーソックス／ハイソックス
knife	*naifu*	ナイフ
knit	*amu*	編む
know	*shiru*	知る

L

lace	*raysu*	レース
lace (shoes)	*kuts-himo*	靴ひも
ladies' room	*fujin-yoh toy-ray*	婦人用トイレ
lake	*mizu-umi*	湖
lamp	*ramp*	ランプ
land (ground)	*tochi*	土地
land (verb)	*chaku-riku suru*	着陸する
lane (of traffic)	*shasen*	車線
language	*kotoba/gengo*	言葉／言語
laptop computer	*rap-pu top-pu*	ラップトップ
large	*ohkee*	大きい
last	*sai-go/sai-shoo*	最後／最終
last night	*sakuban*	昨晩
late	*oso-i*	遅い
later	*nochi hodo*	後程
laugh	*wara-u*	笑う
launderette	*koyn-randoree*	コインランドリー
law	*hohrits*	法律
lawyer	*ben-goshi*	弁護士

laxative	ge-zai	下剤
leak (air)	panku	パンク
leather	kawa	皮
leather goods	kawa-say-hin	皮製品
leave	shuppats suru	出発する
leek	naga-negi	長ネギ
left	hidari	左
left (to turn)	hidari ni magaru	左に曲がる
leg	ashi	足
lemon	remon	レモン
lend	... ni kasu	…に貸す
lens	renz	レンズ
less	sku-naku	少なく
lesson	ressun	レッスン
letter	tegami	手紙
lettuce	retasu	レタス
library	toshokan	図書館
lie	uso	うそ
lie (down)	yoko ni naru	横になる
lie (to tell a)	uso o tsuku	うそをつく
lift (hitchhike)	hit-chi-hai-ku	ヒッチハイク
lift (ski)	rifto	リフト
light	rai-to	ライト
light (not dark)	aka-rui	明るい
light (not heavy)	ka-rui	軽い
lighter	rai-tah	ライター
lighthouse	toh-dai	灯台
lightning	inazuma/ina-bikari/kaminari	稲妻／稲光／かみなり
like (verb)	konomu/ski	好む／好き
line	sen	線
linen	asa/rinen	麻／リネン
lipstick	kuchi-beni	口紅
liquor store	saka-ya	酒屋
liqueur	rikyooru	リキュール
listen	kiku	聞く
literature	bun-gaku	文学
liter	rittoru	リットル
little (amount)	sku-nai	少ない
live	sumu	住む
lobster	isay-ebi	伊勢えび
lock	kagi/johma-e	鍵／錠前
log off	rogu-ofu	ログオフ
log on	rogu-on	ログオン
log-in page	rogu-in-peh-ji	ログインページ
long	na-gai	長い
long distance call	choh-kyori denwa	長距離電話
look	miru	見る
look for	sagasu	捜す
look up	shiraberu	調べる
lose (verb)	ushina-u/nakusu	失う／なくす
loss	sonshits	損失
lost	ushinatta	失った

lost (to be)	*michi ni mayo-u*	道に迷う
lost item	*ish-tsu-buts*	遺失物
lost and found office	*ish-tsu-buts tori-atsu-kai-jo*	遺失物取扱所
lotion	*rohshon*	ローション
loud (voice)	*ohgo-e-de*	大声で
love	*ai/ai-joh*	愛／愛情
love (verb)	*ai-suru*	愛する
love with (to be in)	*ai-shtay iru*	愛している
low	*hiku-i*	低い
low tide	*kanchoh/hiki-shio*	干潮／引き潮
luck	*koh-un*	幸運
luggage	*nimots*	荷物
luggage locker	*koyn-rokkah*	コイン・ロッカー
lumps (sugar)	*kaku-zatoh*	角砂糖
lunch	*choo-shoku*	昼食
lunch room (café)	*koh-hee-shoppu/kissaten*	コーヒーショップ／喫茶店
lungs	*hai*	肺

M

macaroni	*makaroni*	マカロニ
madam	*...-san*	…さん
magazine	*zasshi*	雑誌
maid café	*maido-kafe*	メイドカフェ
mail	*yoobin*	郵便
mailman	*yoobin-ya-san*	郵便屋さん
main post office	*yoobin-kyoku hon-kyoku/ choo-oh yoobin-kyoku*	郵便局本局／中央郵便局
main road	*ohdohri*	大通り
make an appointment	*yak-soku suru*	約束する
make love	*sekks suru*	セックスする
makeshift	*ichiji-teki na*	一時的な
malware	*maru-wea*	マルウェア
man	*otoko*	男
manager (caretaker)	*kanri-nin*	管理人
mandarin orange (fruit)	*mikan*	ミカン
manicure	*manikyua*	マニキュア
many	*tak-san*	たくさん
map	*chizu*	地図
marble	*dai-ri-seki*	大理石
March	*San-gats*	三月
margarine	*mahgarin*	マーガリン
marina	*yotto-yoh dokku/mareena*	ヨット用ドック／マリーナ
market	*ichiba/mahketto*	市場／マーケット
marriage	*kekkon*	結婚
married	*kekkon shta*	結婚した
Mass	*Misa*	ミサ
massage	*massahji*	マッサージ
match	*shi-ai*	試合
matches	*matchi*	マッチ
matte (photo)	*kohtaku no nai*	光沢のない
May	*Go-gats*	五月
maybe	*tabun*	多分
mayonnaise	*mayonehzu*	マヨネーズ

mayor	*shi-choh*	市長
meal	*shokuji*	食事
mean (verb)	*imi suru*	意味する
meat	*niku*	肉
medication	*kusuri/yakuhin*	薬／薬品
medicine	*yakuhin/kusuri*	薬品／薬
meet	*... ni au*	…に会う
melon	*meron*	メロン
melon (water)	*sweeka*	西瓜
membership (card)	*kai-in-shoh*	会員証
menstruate	*gekkay-ga-aru*	月経がある
menstruation	*sayri/mensu*	生理／メンス
menu	*menyoo/kondatay*	メニュー／献立
menu of the day	*honjits no menyoo*	本日のメニュー
message	*dengon*	伝言
metal	*kinzoku*	金属
metal detector	*kinzoku tanchi ki*	金属探知機
meter (in taxi)	*mehtah*	メーター
meter (100 cm)	*meh-toru*	メートル
migraine	*henzutsoo*	偏頭痛
mild (tobacco)	*karui*	軽い
milk	*gyoo-nyoo/miruku*	牛乳／ミルク
millimeter	*miri (meh-toru)*	ミリ（メートル）
mineral water	*mineraru-wohtah*	ミネラルウォーター
minute	*fun*	分
mirror	*kagami*	鏡
miss (a person)	*sabishku-naru*	寂しくなる
missing (to be)	*fusoku suru*	不足する
missing person	*mai-go*	迷子
mistake	*machi-gai*	間違い
mistaken (to be)	*machi-ga-eru*	間違える
misunderstanding	*go-kai*	誤解
mixed-baths	*kon-yoku*	混浴
mixture (medicine)	*nomi-gusuri*	飲み薬
mobile banking	*mobairu-ban-king*	モバイルバンキング
mocha	*moka*	モカ
modern art	*gen-dai gay-juts*	現代芸術
molar	*okuba*	奥歯
moment	*shunkan*	瞬間
moment (just a)	*chotto*	ちょっと
monastery	*shoodoh-in*	修道院
Monday	*Gets-yohbi*	月曜日
money	*o-kanay*	お金
month	*tsuki*	月
moped	*gentsuki-baik*	原付バイク
motel	*mohteru*	モーテル
mother (others')	*o-kah-sama*	お母さま
mother (own)	*haha/o-kah-san*	母／お母さん
motor cross	*moto-kurosu*	モトクロス
motorbike	*baik*	バイク
motorboat	*mohtah-bohto*	モーターボート
mountain	*yama*	山
mountain climbing	*tozan*	登山

mouse	*nezumi*	ネズミ
mouse (computer's)	*mausu*	マウス
mouth	*kuchi*	口
much	*tak-san*	たくさん
muscle	*suji*	筋
muscle spasms	*kinniku no kayren*	筋肉のけいれん
museum	*bijuts-kan/hakubuts-kan*	美術館／博物館
mushrooms	*kinoko*	キノコ
music	*on-gaku*	音楽
musical	*myoojikaru*	ミュージカル
mussels	*mooru-gai*	ムール貝
mustard	*karashi/mastahdo*	からし／マスタード

N

nail	*kugi*	釘
nail (finger)	*tsumay*	つめ
nail file	*tsumay-yasuri*	爪やすり
nail scissors	*tsumay-kiri*	つめ切り
naked	*hadaka/noodo*	裸／ヌード
nationality	*koku-seki*	国籍
natural	*shizen no*	自然の
nature	*shizen*	自然
nauseous	*kibun ga waru-i*	気分が悪い
near	*... no chikaku ni*	…の近くに
nearby	*goku-chikaku no/kinjo no*	ごく近くの／近所の
necessary	*... ga hits-yoh*	…が必要
neck	*kubi*	首
necklace	*nekku-res*	ネックレス
needle	*hari*	針
negative (photo)	*nega*	ネガ
neighbors	*tonari no hito*	隣の人
nephew	*oi*	甥
never	*zenzen/mattaku ... nai*	全然／全く…ない
new	*atara-shee*	新しい
news	*nyoos*	ニュース
news stand	*kiosk/bai-ten*	キオスク／売店
newspaper	*shimbun*	新聞
next	*tsugi no*	次の
next to	*... no soba-ni*	…のそばに
nice	*tanoshee/kai-teki na*	楽しい／快適な
nice (friendly)	*shin-sets*	親切
nice (happy)	*ureshee*	うれしい
nice (person)	*kawa-ee/yoi*	かわいい／よい
nice (taste)	*oi-shee*	おいしい
niece	*may*	姪
night	*yoru*	夜
night duty	*yakin*	夜勤
nightclub	*naito-kurabu*	ナイト・クラブ
nipple (bottle)	*chi-kubi*	乳首
no	*ee-ye*	いいえ
no passing	*oi-koshi kinshi*	追い越し禁止
noise	*uru-sai/soh-on*	うるさい／騒音

non-smoking	*kin-en*	禁煙
nonstop (plane)	*chokkoh*	直行
no one	*daray mo … nai*	だれも…ない
normal	*futsoo*	普通
north	*kita*	北
nose	*hana*	鼻
nose drops	*tem-bi-yaku*	点鼻薬
notepaper	*binsen*	便箋
nothing	*nani-mo … nai*	何も…ない
November	*Joo-ichi-gats*	十一月
nowhere	*doko-nimo … nai*	どこにも…ない
nude beach	*noodisto beech*	ヌーディスト・ビーチ
number	*ban-goh*	番号
number plate	*nambah-purayto*	ナンバー・プレート
nurse	*kangofu*	看護婦
nuts	*natts/otsumami*	ナッツ／おつまみ

O

October	*Joo-gats*	十月
off (gone bad)	*kusatta*	くさった
offer	*mohshi-deru*	申し出る
office	*jimusho/ofiss*	事務所／オフィス
oil	*abura/oiru*	油／オイル
oil level	*oiru no ryoh*	オイルの量
ointment	*nankoh*	軟膏
ointment for burns	*yakedo no nanko*	火傷の軟膏
okay	*OK*	OK
old (thing/person)	*furui/toshi-totta*	古い／年とった
olive oil	*oreebu-yoo*	オリーブ油
olives	*oreebu*	オリーブ
omelette	*omurets*	オムレツ
on	*… no ue ni*	…の上に
on board (to go)	*johsen suru*	乗船する
on the right	*migi no hoh ni*	右の方に
on the way	*tochoo de*	途中で
oncoming car	*tai-koh-sha*	対向車
one-way traffic	*ip-poh tsookoh*	一方通行
onion	*tama-negi*	玉ねぎ
open (to be)	*aitay-iru*	開いている
open (verb)	*akeru*	開ける
open-air bath	*rotem-buro*	露天風呂
opera	*opera*	オペラ
operate (surgeon)	*shujuts suru*	手術する
operator (telephone)	*kohkanshu*	交換手
opposite	*mukoh-gawa*	向こう側
optician	*megane-ya*	眼鏡屋
orange	*orenji*	オレンジ
orange (color)	*orenji-iro*	オレンジ色
orange juice	*orenji-joosu*	オレンジ・ジュース
order	*choomon*	注文
order (tidy)	*kata-zuita*	片づいた
order (verb)	*choomon suru*	注文する

otaku shop	*otaku-shoppu*	オタクショップ
other	*hoka no*	他の
other side	*mukoh-gawa*	向こう側
outside	*soto*	外
overpass	*kohka-kyoh*	高架橋
over there	*asoko*	あそこ
overtake	*oi-kosu*	追い越す
oysters	*kaki*	カキ

P

pacemaker	*peh-su may-kah*	ペースメーカー
packed lunch	*bentoh*	弁当
page	*peh-ji*	ページ
pain	*itami*	痛み
painkiller	*itami-domay/chin-tsoo-zai*	痛み止め／鎮痛剤
paint	*penki*	ペンキ
painting	*kai-ga*	絵画
pajamas	*pajyama*	パジャマ
palace	*kyooden/kohkyo*	宮殿／皇居
pan	*nabay*	鍋
pancake	*pan-kehki*	パンケーキ
pancake (Japanese style)	*hotto-kehki*	ホットケーキ
pane	*mado-garas*	窓ガラス
pants	*zubon/surakks*	ズボン／スラックス
paper	*kami*	紙
parasol	*higasa*	日傘
parcel	*ko-zutsu-mi*	小包み
pardon	*sumimasen*	すみません
parents (others')	*go-ryohshin*	ご両親
parents (own)	*ryohshin*	両親
park	*koh-en*	公園
park (verb)	*choosha suru*	駐車する
parking garage	*choosha-jo*	駐車場
parking space (meter)	*choosha mehtah*	駐車メーター
parsley	*paseri*	パセリ
part (car-)	*buhin*	部品
partner	*koi-bito*	恋人
party	*pahtay*	パーティー
passable (road)	*tsoo-koh dekiru*	通行出来る
passenger	*ryokyaku*	旅客
passport	*pasupohto*	パスポート
passport photo	*shohmay shashin*	証明写真
password	*pasu-wahdo*	パスワード
patient	*byohnin*	病人
pavement	*hodoh*	歩道
pay	*hara-u*	払う
pay the bill	*kanjoh o hara-u*	勘定を払う
peach	*momo*	桃
peanuts	*pee-natts*	ピーナッツ
pear	*nashi*	梨
peas	*gureen-peesu*	グリーンピース
pedal	*pedaru*	ペダル

pedestrian crossing	*ohdan-hodoh*	横断歩道
pedicure	*pedikyua*	ペディキュア
pen	*pen*	ペン
pencil	*empits*	鉛筆
pepper	*koshoh*	胡椒
performance	*joh-en*	上演
perfume	*kohswee*	香水
perm (hair)	*pahma (nento)*	パーマ（ネント）
perm (verb)	*pahma o kakeru*	パーマをかける
permit	*kyoka-sho*	許可書
person	*...-nin*	…人
personal	*kojinteki*	個人的
pets	*petto*	ペット
pharmacy	*yak-kyok*	薬局
phone (tele-)	*denwa*	電話
phone (verb)	*denwa o kakeru*	電話をかける
phone booth	*denwa bokks*	電話ボックス
phone directory	*denwa-choh*	電話帳
photo-editing	*gazoh shori*	画像処理
phone number	*denwa-ban-goh*	電話番号
photo	*shashin*	写真
photocopier	*kopee-ki*	コピー機
photocopy	*kopee*	コピー
photocopy (verb)	*kopee suru*	コピーする
pick up (come to)	*tori ni kuru*	取りに来る
pick up (go to)	*tot-tay kuru*	取って来る
picnic	*piku-nikku*	ピクニック
pier	*fu-toh*	埠頭
pigeon	*hato*	ハト
pill (contraceptive)	*hi-nin-yaku/piru*	避妊薬／ピル
pillow	*makura*	枕
pillowcase	*makura-kabah*	枕カバー
pin	*pin*	ピン
PIN number	*ansho-bangoh*	暗証番号
pineapple	*pai-nap-puru*	パイナップル
pipe	*paipu*	パイプ
pipe tobacco	*paipu-yoh tabako*	パイプ用たばこ
pity	*zannen*	残念
pixel	*gaso*	画素
place of interest	*midokoro/kankoh-chi*	みどころ／観光地
plan	*kay-kaku*	計画
plant	*shokubuts*	植物
plastic	*puraschik*	プラスチック
plastic bag	*bineeru-bukuro*	ビニール袋
plate	*sara*	皿
platform	*(puratto) hohmu*	（プラット）ホーム
play	*geki*	劇
play (verb)	*asobu*	遊ぶ
play golf	*gorufu o suru*	ゴルフをする
play sports	*spohts o suru*	スポーツをする
play tennis	*tenisu o suru*	テニスをする
playground	*yoo-en-chi*	遊園地

playing cards	*torampu*	トランプ
pleasant	*kimochi no-yoi*	気持ちのよい
please	*onegai shimas*	お願いします
pleasure	*tano-shimi*	楽しみ
plum	*umay*	梅
pocketknife	*poketto-naifu*	ポケットナイフ
point	*yubi sasu*	指さす
poison	*doku*	毒
police	*kay-sats*	警察
police station	*kay-sats-sho/kohban*	警察署／交番
policeman	*kaysats-kan/omawari-san*	警察官／おまわりさん
pond	*ikay*	池
pony	*ponee*	ポニー
population	*jinkoh*	人口
pork	*buta-niku*	豚肉
port	*pohto-wain*	ポートワイン
porter (hotel)	*akaboh/pohtah*	赤帽／ポーター
porter	*momban/shu-ay*	門番／守衛
post (zip) code	*yoobin ban-go*	郵便番号
post office	*yoobin-kyoku*	郵便局
postage	*yoobin ryohkin*	郵便料金
postbox	*posto/yoobin bako*	ポスト／郵便箱
postcard	*hagaki/e-hagaki*	葉書／絵葉書
postman	*yoobin-ya-san*	郵便屋さん
potato	*jaga-imo*	ジャガイモ
potato chips	*poteto-chippu*	ポテトチップ
poultry	*kakin*	家禽
powdered milk	*kona-miruku*	粉ミルク
power outlet	*konsento*	コンセント
power spots	*pawah-supotto*	パワースポット
prawns	*ko-ebi*	小エビ
precious	*kichoh*	貴重
prefer	*... hoh ga ski da*	…方が好きだ
preference	*konomi*	好み
pregnant	*nin-shin*	妊娠
prescription	*shohoh*	処方
present (not absent)	*shus-seki*	出席
present (gift)	*purezento*	プレゼント
press	*osu*	押す
pressure	*atsu-ryoku*	圧力
price	*nedan*	値段
price list	*nedan-hyoh*	値段表
print	*printo*	プリント
print (verb)	*printo suru*	プリントする
priority seats	*you-sen seki*	優先席
probably	*tabun*	多分
problem	*mon-dai*	問題
profession	*shoku-gyoh*	職業
program	*program*	プログラム
pronounce	*hatsuon suru*	発音する
pudding (caramel)	*puding/purin*	プディング／プリン
pull	*hiku*	引く

pull a muscle	*kin-niku o itameru*	筋肉を痛める
pulse	*myaku*	脈
pure	*junswee na*	純粋な
purple	*murasaki-iro*	紫色
purse	*hando-bag-gu*	ハンドバッグ
purse (money)	*sai-fu*	サイフ
push	*osu*	押す
puzzle	*nazo/pazuru*	なぞ／パズル

Q

quarter	*yombun-no-ichi*	四分の一
quarter of an hour	*joo-gofun*	十五分
queen	*jo-oh*	女王
question	*shits-mon*	質問
quick	*hayaku*	速く
quiet	*shizuka na*	静かな

R

radio	*rajio*	ラジオ
railways	*tetsudoh*	鉄道
rain	*amay*	雨
rain (verb)	*amay ga furu*	雨が降る
raincoat	*rayn-kohto*	レインコート
rape	*gohkan*	強姦
rapids	*kyooryoo*	急流
raw	*nama no*	生の
raw ham	*nama-hamu*	生ハム
raw vegetables	*nama ya-sai*	生野菜
razor blades	*kamisori*	かみそり
read	*yomu*	読む
ready	*yoh-i no dekita*	用意の出来た
really	*hontoh ni*	ほんとうに
receipt	*ryoh-shuh-sho/uketori-sho*	領収書／受取書
recipe	*chohri-hoh/resipi*	調理法／レシピ
reclining chair	*rikraining chea*	リクライニング・チェア
recommend	*sweesen suru/susumeru*	推薦する／すすめる
rectangle	*choh-hoh-kay*	長方形
red	*a-kai*	赤い
red wine	*aka-wain*	赤ワイン
reduction	*genshoh*	減少
refrigerator	*rayzoh-ko*	冷蔵庫
regards	*... ni yoroshku*	…によろしく
region	*chihoh*	地方
registered	*kaki-tomay*	書留
regular (gasoline)	*regurah*	レギュラー
relatives	*kazoku*	家族
reliable	*tash-ka na*	確かな
religion	*shoo-kyoh*	宗教
rent out	*chin-tai suru*	賃貸する
repair	*shoori o suru*	修理をする
repairs	*shoori*	修理
repeat	*kuri-ka-esu*	繰り返す

report (police)	*choh-sho*	調書
reserve	*yoyaku suru*	予約する
responsible	*sekinin ga aru*	責任がある
rest	*kyookay suru/yasumu*	休憩する／休む
restaurant	*resutoran*	レストラン
result	*kekka*	結果
retired	*tai-shoku shta*	退職した
return (ticket)	*ohfu-ku (kippu)*	往復(切符)
reverse (vehicle)	*bakk suru*	バックする
rheumatism	*ryoomachi*	リューマチ
rice (cooked)	*gohan*	ごはん
rice (grain)	*komay*	米
ridiculous	*baka na/hijoh-shiki na*	ばかな／非常識な
riding (horseback)	*johba*	乗馬
riding school	*johba gakkoh*	乗馬学校
right	*migi*	右
right of way	*yoosen*	優先
ripe	*juku shta*	熟した
risk	*kiken*	危険
river	*kawa*	川
road	*dohro*	道路
roadway	*sha-doh*	車道
rock	*iwa*	岩
roll	*rohru-pan*	ロールパン
roof rack	*roofu-rakku*	ルーフ・ラック
room	*he-ya*	部屋
room number	*he-ya ban-goh*	部屋番号
room service	*room sahbis*	ルーム・サービス
rope	*himo/rohp*	紐／ロープ
rosé (wine)	*rozay*	ロゼ
route	*michi*	道
rowing boat	*bohto*	ボート
rubber	*gomu*	ゴム
rubber band	*wa-gomu*	輪ゴム
rude	*shits-ray na*	失礼な
ruins	*hai-kyo/iseki*	廃虚／遺跡
run into	*... ni de-au*	…に出会う
running shoes	*spohts-shooz*	スポーツ・シューズ

s

sad	*kana-shee*	悲しい
safe (adj.)	*anzen na*	安全な
safe	*kinko*	金庫
safety pin	*anzen-pin*	安全ピン
sail (verb)	*yotto o hashiraseru*	ヨットを走らせる
sailing boat	*yotto*	ヨット
salad	*sarada*	サラダ
salad oil	*sarada-yoo*	サラダ油
salami	*sarami sohsehji*	サラミソーセージ
sale	*uridashi*	売り出し
salt	*shio*	塩
same	*onaji*	同じ

sandy beach	suna-hama	砂浜
sanitary pad	sayri-yoh napkin	生理用ナプキン
sardines	iwashi	イワシ
satisfied	manzoku shta	満足した
Saturday	Do-yohbi	土曜日
sauce	sohsu	ソース
sauna	sauna	サウナ
sausage	sohsehji	ソーセージ
say	yoo	言う
scanner	sukyanah	スキャナー
scarf	skahf/mafurah	スカーフ／マフラー
scenic walk	sampo-michi	散歩道
school	gakkoh	学校
scissors	hasami	はさみ
scooter	skootah	スクーター
Scotch tape	serotehpu	セロテープ
Scotland	Skotto-rando	スコットランド
scrambled eggs	iri-tamago	煎り卵
screen	suku-reen	スクリーン
screw	neji	ねじ
screwdriver	neji-mawashi/doraibah	ねじ回し／ドライバー
sculpture	choh-kok	彫刻
SD card	SD kah-do	SDカード
sea	umi	海
search engine	sah-chi enjin	サーチエンジン
seasick	funa-yoi	船酔い
seat	zaseki	座席
second	byoh	秒
second (in line)	dai-ni	第二
second-hand	chooko-hin	中古品
security	sekyuritee	セキュリティー
sedative	chinsay-zai	鎮静剤
see	miru	見る
see (go sightseeing)	kankoh ni iku	観光に行く
self-catering accommodation	sudomari	素泊まり
self-timer	serufu-taimah	セルフ・タイマー
send	okuru	送る
sentence	bunshoh	文章
September	Ku-gats	九月
serious	shinkoku na	深刻な
service	sahbis	サービス
serviette	napukin	ナプキン
set	setto	セット
sewing needs	sai-hoh dohgu	裁縫道具
shade	kagay	影
shallow	a-sai	浅い
shampoo	shampoo	シャンプー
shark	samay/fu-ka	サメ／フカ
shave	soru	剃る
shaver	shaybah/denki kamisori	シェーバー／電気かみそり
shaving brush	hige-sori-yoh burashi	ひげ剃り用ブラシ

shaving cream	*shay-bing-kureemu*	シェービング・クリーム
shaving soap	*hige-sori-yoh sekken*	ひげ剃り用石けん
sheet	*sheets*	シーツ
sherry	*she-ree-shu*	シェリー酒
shirt	*shats*	シャツ
shoe	*kuts*	靴
shoe polish	*kuts-kureemu*	靴クリーム
shoe shop	*kuts-ya*	靴屋
shoemaker	*kuts-naoshi*	靴直し
shop	*misay*	店
shop (verb)	*kai-mono o suru*	買い物をする
shop assistant	*han-bai-in/ten-in*	販売員／店員
shop window	*shoh-windoh*	ショーウィンドー
shopping center	*shoppingu-sentah*	ショッピングセンター
short	*miji-kai*	短い
short circuit	*shohto*	ショート
shorts	*han-zubon*	半ズボン
shoulder	*kata*	肩
show	*show/joh-en*	ショー／上演
shower	*shawah*	シャワー
shutter	*shattah*	シャッター
sieve	*furui*	ふるい
sign (name)	*sho-may suru*	署名する
sign (road)	*kohtsoo hyoh-shiki*	交通標識
signal/reception for cell phone	*dempa*	電波
signature	*sho-may/sain*	署名／サイン
silence	*chinmoku/shizukesa*	沈黙／静けさ
silver	*gin*	銀
SIM card	*shimu kah-do*	SIMカード
simple	*tanjun na*	単純な
single	*shinguru*	シングル
single (one way)	*katamichi*	片道
single (unmarried)	*dokushin no*	独身の
single-lens reflex (SLR) camera	*ichi-gun-refu kamera*	一眼レフカメラ
sir	*...-san*	…さん
sister (elder, others')	*o-nay-san*	お姉さん
sister (elder, own)	*anay*	姉
sister (younger, others')	*imohto-san*	妹さん
sister (younger, own)	*imohto*	妹
sit	*suwaru*	座る
size	*saizu*	サイズ
ski (verb)	*skee o suru*	スキーをする
ski boots	*skee-guts*	スキー靴
ski goggles	*skee-yoh gohguru*	スキー用ゴーグル
ski instructor	*skee shidoh-in*	スキー指導員
ski lessons/class	*skee ressun/kyoh-shits*	スキーレッスン／教室
ski lift	*skee-rifuto*	スキーリフト
ski pants	*skee-zubon/skee-yoh pants*	スキーズボン／スキー用パンツ
ski pole	*stokku*	ストック
ski slope	*gerenday*	ゲレンデ

ski suit	*skee-soots*	スキースーツ
ski wax	*skee-yoh wakkusu*	スキー用ワックス
skin	*hada*	肌
skirt	*sukahto*	スカート
skis	*skee*	スキー
sleep	*nemuru*	眠る
sleeping car	*shin-dai-sha*	寝台車
sleeping pills	*swee-min-yaku*	睡眠薬
slide	*su-raido*	スライド
slip	*surippu/petikohto*	スリップ／ペティコート
slow	*yuk-kuri*	ゆっくり
slow train	*kaku-eki ressha*	各駅列車
small	*chee-sai*	小さい
small change	*kozeni*	小銭
smart phone	*sumah-to fon/sumaho*	スマートフォン／スマホ
smell	*ni-ou*	臭う
smoke	*kemuri*	煙
smoked	*kunsay shta*	薫製した
smoking	*kitsu-en*	喫煙
smoking compartment	*kitsu-en-sha*	喫煙車
snake	*hebi*	ヘビ
snorkel	*snohkeru*	スノーケル
snow	*yuki*	雪
snow (verb)	*yuki ga furu*	雪が降る
snowboarding	*sunoh boh-do/sunobo*	スノーボード／スノボ
snow chains	*chayn*	チェーン
soap	*sekken*	石けん
soap box	*sekken-bako*	石けん箱
soap powder	*kona-sekken*	粉石けん
soccer	*sakkah*	サッカー
soccer match	*sakkah no shi-ai*	サッカーの試合
social networking	*soh-sharu netto wah-kingu/ es-enu-es*	ソーシャルネットワーキング／SNS
socket	*konsento*	コンセント
socks	*kutsu-shta/sokks*	靴下／ソックス
soft drink	*sofut-dorinku*	ソフト・ドリンク
software	*sofuto-uea*	ソフトウェア
sole (fish)	*shta-biramay*	舌びらめ
sole (shoe)	*kutsu-zoko*	靴底
someone	*daray-ka*	誰か
sometimes	*toki-doki*	時々
somewhere	*doko-ka*	どこか
son (others')	*mus-ko-san*	息子さん
son (own)	*mus-ko*	息子
soon	*hayaku*	早く
sore	*kizu*	傷
sore throat	*nodo no itami*	のどの痛み
sorry	*sumimasen*	すみません
soup	*soop*	スープ
sour	*sup-pai*	すっぱい
sour cream	*sawah-kureemu*	サワークリーム
south	*minami*	南

souvenir	*omiyagay/omiyage-hin*	おみやげ／おみやげ品
soy sauce	*shoh-yu*	醤油
spaghetti	*spagetti*	スパゲッティ
spare	*yobi*	予備
spare parts	*yobi-buhin*	予備部品
speak	*hanasu*	話す
special	*tokubets na*	特別な
specialist (doctor)	*semmon-i*	専門医
speciality (cooking)	*osusume ryohri*	おすすめ料理
speed limit	*sai-koh sokudo*	最高速度
spell	*tsuzuru*	つづる
spicy	*spaishee*	スパイシー
splinter	*togay*	とげ
spoon	*spoon*	スプーン
sport	*spohts*	スポーツ
sports center	*spohts-sentah*	スポーツ・センター
spot (place)	*basho*	場所
sprain	*kujiku*	くじく
spring	*haru*	春
square (plaza)	*hiroba*	広場
square (shape)	*sayhoh-kay*	正方形
square meters	*hayhoh meh-toru*	平方メートル
squash	*skahsh o suru*	スカッシュをする
stadium	*stajiam*	スタジアム
stain	*shimi*	しみ
stain remover	*shimi-tori*	しみ取り
stairs	*kai-dan*	階段
stamp	*kit-tay*	切手
start	*ugoki-dasaseru*	動き出させる
station	*eki*	駅
statue	*zoh*	像
stay (in hotel)	*shuku-haku suru*	宿泊する
stay (remain)	*tai-zai*	滞在
steal	*nusumu*	盗む
steel	*kohtets*	鋼鉄
stench	*ku-sai ni-oi*	臭いにおい
sting (noun)	*mushi-sasaray*	虫さされ
stitch (med.)	*(kizu-o) nui-awaseru*	(傷を)縫い合わせる
stitch (verb)	*noo*	縫う
stock (soup)	*soop no moto/sashi*	スープの素／出汁
stockings	*stokkingu*	ストッキング
stomach	*i*	胃
stomach (abdominal region)	*hara/fukubu*	腹／腹部
stomach ache	*fuku-tsoo*	腹痛
stomach cramps	*hageshee fuku-tsoo*	激しい腹痛
stools	*dai-ben*	大便
stop	*tomaru*	止まる
stop (bus)	*tay-ryoo-jo/tay-sha-jo*	停留所／停車場
stopover	*tochoo-gesha*	途中下車
storm	*arashi*	嵐
straight	*massugu*	真っ直ぐ

straight ahead	*massugu ni*	真っ直ぐに
straw	*sutoroh*	ストロー
strawberries	*ichigo*	イチゴ
street	*michi*	道
street side	*michibata*	道端
strike	*suto (raiki)*	スト（ライキ）
strong	*tsuyo-i*	強い
study	*benkyoh suru*	勉強する
stuffing	*tsu-me-mono*	詰め物
subtitled	*jimaki-tsuki-de*	字幕付きで
subway	*chika*	地くだ
subway station	*chika-tets no eki*	地くだ鉄の駅
subway system	*chika-tets*	地くだ鉄
succeed	*dekiru*	出来る
sugar	*satoh*	砂糖
suit	*soots*	スーツ
suitcase	*soots-kays*	スーツケース
summer	*nats*	夏
sun	*tai-yoh*	太陽
sun hat	*hiyoke-boh*	日よけ帽
sunbathe	*nikkoh-yoku*	日光浴
Sunday	*Nichi-yohbi*	日曜日
sunglasses	*san-guras*	サングラス
sunrise	*hinoday*	日の出
sunset	*higuray*	日暮れ
sunstroke	*nissha-byoh*	日射病
suntan lotion	*hiyakedome kureemu*	日焼け止めクリーム
suntan oil	*san-oiru*	さんけオイル
supermarket	*soopah (mahketto)*	スーパー（マーケット）
surcharge	*tsweeka ryohkin*	追加料金
surf	*sahfin o suru*	サーフィンをする
surf board	*sahfu-bohdo*	サーフボード
surname	*myoh-ji*	苗字
surprise	*odoroki*	驚き
swallow	*nomi-komu*	飲みこむ
swamp	*numa-chi*	沼地
sweat	*asay*	汗
sweater	*sehtah*	セーター
sweet	*ama-i*	甘い
sweet (kind)	*shin-sets na*	親切な
sweet corn	*toh-moro-koshi*	トウモロコシ
swim	*oyogu*	泳ぐ
swimming pool	*pooru*	プール
swimming trunks	*swee-ay pants*	水泳パンツ
swindle	*sagi*	詐欺
switch	*swit-chi*	スイッチ
synagogue	*yudayakyoh no kyohkai*	ユダヤ教の教会
syrup	*shiroppu*	シロップ

T

table	*tehburu*	テーブル
table tennis	*takkyoo/pin-pon*	卓球／ピンポン

tablet	*joh-zai*	錠剤
tablet PC	*taburetto(-gata paso-kon)*	タブレット（型パソコン）
take (medicine)	*fukuyoh suru*	服用する
take (photograph)	*(shashin-o) toru*	（写真を）撮る
take (time)	*jikan ga kakaru*	時間がかかる
talcum powder	*tarukamu paudah*	タルカム・パウダー
talk	*hanasu*	話す
tall	*say ga ta-kai*	背が高い
tampons	*tampon*	タンポン
tanned	*hi ni yaketa*	日に焼けた
tap	*jaguchi*	蛇口
tap water	*sweedoh no mizu*	水道の水
taste (verb)	*tamesu*	試す
taste	*aji*	味
tax free shop	*menzay-ten*	免税店
taxi	*takshee*	タクシー
taxi stand	*takshee noriba*	タクシー乗り場
tea	*ocha*	お茶
tea (black)	*kohcha*	紅茶
tea (green)	*ryokucha*	緑茶
tea ceremony	*ocha-kai*	お茶会
teapot	*kyoosu/tee-pott*	急須／ティーポット
teaspoon	*chasaji/tee-spoon*	茶さじ／ティースプーン
telegram	*dempoh*	電報
telephoto lens	*boh-en renzu*	望遠レンズ
television	*terebi*	テレビ
temperature (body)	*tai-on*	体温
temperature (heat)	*ondo*	温度
temperature (weather)	*kion*	気温
temporary filling	*ichiji-teki na mushiba no tsumemono*	一時的な虫歯の詰め物
tender	*yawara-kai*	柔らかい
tennis ball	*tenisu-bohru*	テニスボール
tennis court	*tenisu-kohto*	テニスコート
tennis racket	*tenisu-raketto*	テニスラケット
tent	*tento*	テント
tent peg	*pegu*	ペグ
terrace	*terasu*	テラス
terribly	*tai-hen na*	大変な
texting	*may-ru*	メール
thank	*oray o yoo*	お礼を言う
thank you	*arigatoh gozai-mas*	ありがとうございます
thanks	*arigatoh*	ありがとう
thaw	*tokeru*	溶ける
the day after tomorrow	*asat-tay*	あさって
theatre	*gekijo*	劇場
theft	*settoh*	窃盗
there	*soko*	そこ
thermal bath	*onsen*	温泉
thermometer (body)	*tai-on-kay*	体温計
thermometer (weather)	*ondo-kay*	温度計
thick	*futo-i*	太い
thief	*doroboh*	泥棒

thigh	*futo-momo*	太腿
thin (not fat)	*hoso-i/yaseta*	細い／痩せた
thin (not thick)	*usu-i*	薄い
think	*omo-u*	思う
think (consider)	*kana-eru*	考える
third (¹/₃)	*sambun no ichi*	三分の一
thirsty (to be)	*nodo ga kawaku*	喉が渇く
this afternoon	*kyoh no gogo*	今日の午後
this evening	*kom-ban*	今晩
this morning	*kyoh no gozen*	今日の午前
thread	*ito*	糸
throat	*nodo*	喉
throat lozenges	*seki-domay doroppu*	せき止めドロップ
throw up	*haku*	吐く
thunderstorm	*rai-u*	雷雨
Thursday	*moku-yohbi*	木曜日
ticket	*kippu*	切符
ticket office (travel)	*midori no mado-guchi*	みどりの窓口
ticket (admission)	*nyoo-joh-ken*	入場券
ticket (travel)	*kippu*	切符
tickets (seat)	*zaseki-ken*	座席券
tidy	*kata-zukeru*	片付ける
tie	*neku-tai*	ネクタイ
tights	*pan-sto*	パンスト
time	*jikan*	時間
times	*kai*	回
timetable	*jikoku-hyoh*	時刻表
tin (canned)	*kanzu-may*	缶詰め
tip	*chippu*	チップ
tire	*tai-ya*	タイヤ
tire pressure	*tai-ya kooki-atsu*	タイヤ空気圧
toast	*tohsto*	トースト
tobacco	*tabako*	たばこ
toboggan	*sori*	そり
today	*kyoh*	今日
toe	*ashi no yubi/tsuma-saki*	足の指／つま先
together	*issho ni*	一緒に
toilet	*toiray/o-te-a-rai/benjo*	トイレ／お手洗い／便所
toilet paper	*toiretto-pehpah*	トイレットペーパー
toiletries	*keshoh-hin*	化粧品
tomato	*tomato*	トマト
tomato puree	*tomato-pyuray*	トマトピュレ
tomato sauce	*tomato-kechappu*	トマトケチャップ
tomorrow	*ashta*	明日
tongue	*shta*	舌
tonight	*kom-ban/kon'ya*	今晩／今夜
tools	*doh-gu*	道具
tooth	*ha*	歯
toothache	*ha-ita, shi-tsoo*	歯痛
toothbrush	*ha-burashi*	歯ブラシ
toothpaste	*ha-migaki*	歯磨
toothpick	*yohji*	ようじ

top up	*okawari*	おかわり
total	*zem-bu*	全部
tough	*ka-tai*	固い
tour	*tsu-ah/shoo-yoo/ryokoh*	ツアー／周遊／旅行
tour guide	*an-nai-sha/gaido*	案内者／ガイド
tourist class	*ni-toh*	二等
Tourist Information office	*Kankoh an-nai-sho*	観光案内所
tow	*ken-in suru*	牽引する
tow cable	*ken-in rohpu*	牽引ロープ
towel	*ta-oru/te-nugui*	タオル／手拭い
tower	*toh*	塔
town	*machi*	町
town hall	*shiyaku-sho*	市役所
toys	*omocha*	おもちゃ
traffic	*kohtsoo*	交通
traffic light	*shingo*	信号
train	*ressha*	列車
train (electric)	*densha*	電車
train ticket	*kippu*	切符
train timetable	*jikoku-hyoh*	時刻表
translate	*hon-yaku suru*	翻訳する
travel	*ryokoh suru*	旅行する
travel agent	*ryokoh-dairi-ten*	旅行代理店
travel guide	*ryokoh an-nai/an-nai-sho*	旅行案内／案内書
traveler	*ryokoh-sha*	旅行者
traveler's check	*ryokoh-yoh kogit-tay*	旅行用小切手
treatment	*chi-ryoh*	治療
triangle	*sankaku*	三角
trim	*kiri-soro-eru*	切りそろえる
trip	*ryokoh*	旅行
trip (sightseeing)	*kankoh*	観光
trip (walk)	*sampo*	散歩
trout	*masu*	マス（鱒）
truck	*trakku*	トラック
trustworthy	*tayori ni naru*	たよりになる
try on	*shichaku suru*	試着する
tube	*choob*	チューブ
Tuesday	*Ka-yohbi*	火曜日
tuna	*maguro*	マグロ
tunnel	*tonneru*	トンネル
turn	*kai*	回
TV	*terebi*	テレビ
TV guide	*terebi gai-do*	テレビガイド
tweet	*tsuee-to/tsubuyaki*	ツイート/つぶやき
tweezers	*pinsetto*	ピンセット
typhoon	*tai-foo*	台風

U

ugly	*minikui/utsu-kushiku-nai*	みにくい／美しくない
umbrella	*kasa*	傘
under	*... no shta-ni*	…のくだに
underpants	*pants*	パンツ

understand	*wakaru/ri-kai suru*	分かる／理解する
underwear	*shta-gi*	下着
undress	*fuku o nugu*	服を脱ぐ
unemployed	*shits-gyoh*	失業
uneven (ground)	*dekoboko no*	でこぼこの
university	*dai-gaku*	大学
unleaded	*mu-en/regyurah-gasorin*	無鉛／レギュラーガソリン
up	*ue*	上
upload	*up-roh-do*	アップロード
urgent	*hijoh/kinkyoo*	非常／緊急
urgently	*sohkyoo-ni*	早急に
urine	*shohben/oshikko*	小便／おしっこ
used bookstore	*furu-hon ya*	古本屋
username	*yoo-zah-may*	ユーザー名
usually	*tai-tay*	たいてい

V

vacate	*tachi-noku*	立ち退く
vaccinate	*yoboh sesshu*	予防接種
vagina	*chits*	膣
valid	*kachi no aru*	価値のある
valley	*tani*	谷
valuable	*kohka na*	高価な
van	*raito-ban/wagon-sha/ minibas*	ライトバン／ワゴン車／ ミニバス
vanilla	*banira*	バニラ
vase	*kabin*	花瓶
veal	*ko-ushi no niku*	子牛の肉
vegetable soup	*ya-sai soop*	野菜スープ
vegetables	*ya-sai*	野菜
vegetarian	*bejitarian/sai-shok-ka*	ベジタリアン／菜食家
vein	*joh-myaku*	静脈
vending machine	*jidoh ham-bai-ki*	自動販売機
venereal disease	*say-byoh*	性病
via	*kay-yoo*	経由
video	*doh-ga*	動画
video camera	*bideo-kamera*	ビデオ・カメラ
video recorder	*bideo-rekohdah*	ビデオレコーダー
video tape	*bideo-tehpu*	ビデオテープ
view	*nagamay*	眺め
village	*mura*	村
virus	*ui-rusu*	ウィルス
visa	*biza*	ビザ
visit	*hohmon suru*	訪問する
visiting card	*may-shi*	名刺
visiting time	*menkai jikan*	面会時間
vitamin tablets	*bitamin-zai*	ビタミン剤
vitamins	*bitamin*	ビタミン
volcano	*kazan*	火山
volleyball	*baray-bohru*	バレーボール
vomit	*haku/modosu*	吐く／戻す

W

English	Romaji	Japanese
wait	*mats*	待つ
waiter	*waytah*	ウェーター
waiting room	*machi-a-i-shits*	待合室
waitress	*waytresu*	ウェイトレス
wake up	*okiru*	起きる
Wales	*wayruzu*	ウェールズ
walk (noun)	*sampo*	散歩
walk (verb)	*sampo suru/aruku*	散歩する／歩く
wallet	*saifu*	財布
warm	*atatakai*	温かい
warn	*choo-i suru*	注意する
warning	*choo-i*	注意
wash	*ara-u*	洗う
washing	*sentaku-mono*	洗濯物
washing machine	*sentak-ki*	洗濯機
wasp	*suzume-bachi*	スズメバチ
watch	*uday-do-kay*	腕時計
water	*mizu*	水
water ski	*sweejoh skee o suru*	水上スキーをする
watermill	*sweesha*	水車
waterproof	*bohswee*	防水
wave-pool	*jinkoh-ha pooru/nami no pooru*	人工波プール／波のプール
way (direction)	*hohmen*	方面
way (method)	*shudan/hoh-hoh*	手段／方法
we	*watash-tachi*	私達
weak	*yowa-i*	弱い
weather	*tenki*	天気
weather forecast	*tenki yo-hoh*	天気予報
Web site	*webu-sait*	ウェブサイト
wedding	*kekkon-shki*	結婚式
Wednesday	*Swee-yohbi*	水曜日
week	*shoo*	週
weekend	*shoo-mats*	週末
weekly ticket	*isshookan no tayki-ken*	一週間の定期券
welcome	*irassha-i*	いらっしゃい
well (good)	*ee/yoi*	いい／良い
well (water)	*ido*	井戸
west	*nishi*	西
wet	*nureta*	濡れた
wetsuit	*wetto-soots*	ウェット・スーツ
what	*nani*	何
wheel	*sharin*	車輪
wheelchair	*kuruma-isu*	車いす
when	*its*	いつ
where	*doko*	どこ
which	*dochira*	どちら
white	*shiro-i*	白い
who	*daray*	誰
why	*nazay*	なぜ
wide-angle lens	*kohkaku renzu*	広角レンズ

15

widow	*mibohjin*	未亡人
widower	*otoko-yamomay*	男やもめ
wife (others')	*okusama*	奥さま
wife (own)	*tsuma*	妻
Wi-Fi	*musen-ran/Wai-Fai*	無線LAN／Wi-Fi
Wi-Fi built-in digital camera	*Wai-Fai toh-sai deji-kame*	Wi-Fi 搭載デジカメ
wind	*kazay*	風
windbreak	*kazay-yokay*	風よけ
windmill	*foosha*	風車
window	*mado*	窓
window (of ticket office)	*mado-guchi*	窓口
windshield wiper	*wai-pah*	ワイパー
wine	*wa-in*	ワイン
wine list	*wa-in risuto*	ワインリスト
wine shop	*saka-ya*	酒屋
winter	*fuyu*	冬
witness	*shoh-nin*	証人
woman	*on'na*	女
wonderful (taste)	*oy-shee*	おいしい
wood	*ki*	木
wool (for knitting)	*kay-to*	毛糸
word	*kotoba*	言葉
work	*shi-goto*	仕事
worn	*furuku-natta*	古くなった
worried	*shimpai na*	心配な
wound	*kizu*	傷
wrap	*tsutsumu*	包む
wrist	*tekubi*	手首
write	*kaku*	書く
write down	*kaki-tomeru/kiroku suru*	書き留める／記録する
writing pad/paper	*binsen*	便箋
wrong	*machi-gatta*	間違った

Y

yacht	*yotto*	ヨット
year	*toshi/nen*	年
yellow	*kee-roy*	黄色い
yes	*hai*	はい
yes, please	*hai, itadaki-mas/onegai shimas*	はい、いただきます／お願いします
yesterday	*kinoh*	昨日
yoga	*yoga*	ヨガ
yogurt	*yohguruto*	ヨーグルト
you	*anata*	あなた
you too	*anata mo*	あなたも
youth hostel	*yoos-hosteru*	ユースホステル

Z

zip	*fasunah/jip-pah*	ファスナー／ジッパー
zoo	*doh-butsu-en*	動物園
zucchini	*zuk-keeni*	ズッキーニ

"Books to Span the East and West"

Tuttle Publishing was founded in 1832 in the small New England town of Rutland, Vermont [USA]. Our core values remain as strong today as they were then—to publish best-in-class books which bring people together one page at a time. In 1948, we established a publishing office in Japan—and Tuttle is now a leader in publishing English-language books about the arts, languages and cultures of Asia. The world has become a much smaller place today and Asia's economic and cultural influence has grown. Yet the need for meaningful dialogue and information about this diverse region has never been greater. Over the past seven decades, Tuttle has published thousands of books on subjects ranging from martial arts and paper crafts to language learning and literature—and our talented authors, illustrators, designers and photographers have won many prestigious awards. We welcome you to explore the wealth of information available on Asia at www.tuttlepublishing.com.

Published by Tuttle Publishing, an imprint of Periplus Editions (HK) Ltd.

www.tuttlepublishing.com

Copyright © 2017 Periplus Editions (HK) Ltd.

Library of Congress Control Number: 2012932262
This edition ISBN 978-4-8053-1444-9
(Previously published with ISBN 978-0-8048-4243-3)

ISBN 978-4-8053-1444-9

First edition
26 25 24 23   11 10 9 8 7   2211MP
Printed in Singapore

TUTTLE PUBLISHING® is a registered trademark of Tuttle Publishing, a division of Periplus Editions (HK) Ltd.

Distributed by

North America, Latin America & Europe
Tuttle Publishing
364 Innovation Drive
North Clarendon
VT 05759-9436 U.S.A.
Tel: 1 (802) 773-8930
Fax: 1 (802) 773-6993
info@tuttlepublishing.com
www.tuttlepublishing.com

Japan
Tuttle Publishing
Yaekari Building 3rd Floor 5-4-12 Osaki
Shinagawa-ku
Tokyo 141 0032
Tel: (81) 3 5437-0171
Fax: (81) 3 5437-0755
sales@tuttle.co.jp
www.tuttle.co.jp

Asia Pacific
Berkeley Books Pte. Ltd.
3 Kallang Sector #04-01
Singapore 349278
Tel: (65) 6741-2178
Fax: (65) 6741-2179
inquiries@periplus.com.sg
www.tuttlepublishing.com